CLASSICAL LITERARY CRITICISM

Aristotle was born in Stageira in 384 B.C., in the dominion of the Macedonian kings. He studied in Athens under Plato, leaving on his death, and some time later became tutor to the young Alexander the Great. On Alexander's succession to the throne in 335 B.C., Aristotle returned to Athens and established the Lyceum, where his vast erudition attracted a large number of scholars. After Alexander's death he was regarded in some quarters with suspicion, because he had been known as Alexander's friend. He was accused of impiety, and consequently fled to Chalcis in Euboea, where he died in the same year. His writings covered an extremely wide range of subjects, and fortunately many of them have survived. Among the most famous are the *Ethics* and the *Politics*. These have both been published in Penguin Classics.

Horace, the Latin lyric poet and satirist, was born in Venusia in Apulia in about 65 B.C. He was educated in Rome and Athens. In 44 B.C. Horace enlisted in Brutus's army and fought at Philippi as a military tribune. Ensuing poverty, he says, drove him to write poetry. Horace is said to be the most quoted author of antiquity, appealing to a wider range of readers of every age and at any age than any other ancient poet. His *Odes*, *Epodes* and *Satires* have also been published in Penguin Classics.

It has been thought that the treatise *On the Sublime* was written by Cassius Longinus, who was a 3rd-century B.C. Greek rhetorician, minister of Zenobia, queen of Palmyra. However, it is now generally ascribed to an unknown Greek author writing in the mid 1st century B.C.

•

T. S. Dorsch was Professor of English at the University of Durham from 1968 until his retirement in 1976. He also taught at Westfield College, University of London, where he was Reader. Among his publications is the Shakespeare section in *The New Cambridge Bibliography of English Literature* (1974).

CLASSICAL LITERARY CRITICISM

ARISTOTLE: *On the Art of Poetry*
HORACE: *On the Art of Poetry*
LONGINUS: *On the Sublime*

TRANSLATED WITH
AN INTRODUCTION BY

T. S. Dorsch

PENGUIN BOOKS

Penguin Books Ltd, Harmondsworth, Middlesex, England
Viking Penguin Inc., 40 West 23rd Street, New York, New York 10010, U.S.A.
Penguin Books Australia Ltd, Ringwood, Victoria, Australia
Penguin Books Canada Limited, 2801 John Street, Markham, Ontario, Canada L3R 1B4
Penguin Books (N.Z.) Ltd, 182–190 Wairau Road, Auckland 10, New Zealand

—

This translation first published in 1965
Reprinted 1967, 1969, 1970, 1972, 1974, 1975, 1977, 1978, 1979,
1981, 1982, 1983, 1984, 1986

—

—

Set, printed and bound in Great Britain by
Cox & Wyman Ltd, Reading
Set in Monotype Garamond

Contents

Introduction

THE translations in this volume begin with Aristotle's *Poetics*. But literary criticism, as the term is understood today, did not come into being with Aristotle, any more than epic poetry came into being with the Homeric poems or English poetry with Chaucer. A very rudimentary form of literary criticism may perhaps be discerned already in Homer and Hesiod, both of whom regard poetry as the product of divine inspiration; for Homer its function is to give pleasure, for Hesiod to give instruction, to pass on the message breathed into the poet by the Muse. A few literary pronouncements are scattered through the odes of Pindar, and the philosophers Xenophanes and Heraclitus both find fault with passages of Homer. Discussion of these first stirrings of the critical faculty will be found in the first volume of J. W. H. Atkins's *Literary Criticism in Antiquity* (Methuen, 1952). However, nothing more than a handful of sketchy comments on poets and poetry emerges from these early periods.

With Aristophanes we enter into a different world. In most of his eleven extant plays, which were produced in the last quarter of the fifth and the early years of the fourth centuries B.C., the writers and thinkers of his own age and of the immediately preceding age figure, often very prominently, among the objects of his satire. In *The Clouds*, for example, he takes Socrates as the leading representative of the New Learning of the day, and, by the method of *reductio ad absurdum*, makes fun of him and of his techniques of argument and instruction. In *The Birds* he has much to say about contemporary lyrical poetry, and in *The Wasps* something about contemporary comedy.

However, Euripides is the principal object of Aristophanes' literary satire. By some of his contemporaries Euripides was considered to be lowering the dignity of tragedy by his fondness for maimed and diseased and 'low' characters and for 'low' diction, and in *The Acharnians*, the first of Aristophanes' surviving plays, written some twenty years before the death of Euripides, the latter is depicted as a purveyor of rag-bag language and rag-bag characters, and is induced to part with some of his rags in the shape of phrases from his plays. In the *Thesmophoriazusae* he incurs the anger of the women of Athens for having traduced their sex in his plays, and is made to appear in some ridiculous situations. And he is known to have been the main object of satire in the *Proagon*, one of the lost plays of Aristophanes. Finally, as most readers will know, the second half of *The Frogs* concerns an attempt by Euripides to oust Aeschylus from the throne of tragedy in Hades. A contest between the two poets is arranged, with Dionysus as judge, and they alternately spout lines from their plays which Dionysus weighs in a pair of scales. Although he has to give ground on a few artistic points, Aeschylus emerges as the 'weightier' poet, especially in subject-matter, and after the final round, in which the question at issue is the soundness of the political advice imparted by each of them, Aeschylus is adjudged the clear winner. In the course of the dispute many weaknesses and idiosyncrasies of the two poets are laid bare; at the same time Aristophanes shows that he is well aware of their many excellences.

For, in spite of the ridicule that he heaps upon him in the various plays in which he appears, it must not be supposed that Aristophanes is merely the detractor of Euripides. Indeed, it is clear that, although there are elements in his plays of which he disapproves, he actually admires him. His admiration is most obviously manifested in his intimate familiarity with the plays of Euripides, a familiarity which enables him always to select the most telling lines or phrases to use against him. Furthermore, while Aristophanes freely employs scurrility and abuse in exposing the vice and the evil motives of those whom he hates or despises – Cleon, for example, and the military and political leaders generally – he is always good-humoured in his treatment of Euripides. He never calls in question his reputation or integrity or personal qualities, as he so often does with those whom he dislikes; and his satire of him in *The Frogs* is interspersed with what may be interpreted as praise of some of his artistic merits. He grants, in effect, that Euripides has clarified tragedy by his skilful use of prologues which explain details and give a clear picture of anterior events; that he has a feeling for dialogue, in contrast with what might almost be called the set-speech method of Aeschylus; and that his realism and rationalism bring tragedy into a closer touch with real life than had been achieved by earlier poets. Indeed, in matters relating to the art and craft of tragedy he allows him some slight superiority over Aeschylus. His criticism is much broader in scope and less one-sided in intention than is sometimes suggested.

This is not the place for a full-scale study of Aristophanes' criticism, but a few general conclusions may be drawn. In his plays, especially *The Frogs*, he displays a well-developed taste and a keen insight in his literary judgements. He does not attempt anything like a full estimate of the authors whom he treats, not even of Euripides, but his views are always grounded in good sense, and are presented more concretely, perhaps, than those of any other critic until comparatively recent times; they are concretely presented not only by reason of his setting his authors before us to reveal themselves, but also by his methods of selective quotation with attendant comments, and of brilliantly perceptive parody, which in combination amount to something not unlike the modern analysis of texts. It is not possible, I think, to draw his judgements together into a clearly-defined critical code. However, he is consistent in his dislike of excesses and affectations of any kind, and he brings out a fundamental aspect of literary criticism in the importance that he attaches to moral values in the judgement of literature. He is a very important figure in the early history of literary criticism.

That other comic playwrights contemporary with and later than Aristophanes were also fond of literary subjects is suggested by several play-titles that have come down to us. For example, Cratinus, who in fact was born about seventy-five years before Aristophanes, wrote a play entitled *Archilochoi*, which had a chorus of Archilochuses. Archilochus of Paros, who flourished at the turn of the eighth and seventh centuries, was a poet of very high repute among the ancients; among other things, he is generally credited with the establishment of satire as a literary genre, and he was held up as the type of the severe critic. It may be presumed that a play in which the chorus was made up of Archilochuses contained literary satire, perhaps of much the same kind as Aristophanes wrote. Other titles that have survived include *The Poet, The Muses, Sappho, The Rehearsal,* and *Heracles the Stage-Manager*; but as these plays are lost, nothing can be said about the way in which they treated literary topics. A fragment remains from a play entitled *Poetry*, written by Antiphanes probably about the middle of the fourth century; it concerns the relative difficulties of writing tragedy and comedy.

It is not easy to write briefly about Plato's contribution to literary criticism. His literary judgements are scattered through seven or eight of his Socratic dialogues, and are invariably subordinated to topics – ethical, metaphysical, political, or educational – which are more fundamental to the particular theses that he is at the time developing. Plato's active career coincides almost exactly with the first half of the fourth century.

Everyone knows that Plato attacked poets and poetry, and excluded poets from his ideal republic. It is not so generally known that he attacked them only for particular reasons and in particular contexts. He himself wrote poetry, and wrote very poetically in his prose works; and although there were qualities in much existing poetry of which he did not approve, it is clear from many remarks in the dialogues that, generally speaking, he found much pleasure in poetry. In *The Republic*, where his so-called attack is most fully developed, his main preoccupations are political, not artistic. He banishes literature and the arts because they have no political utility, and may indeed exert an adverse influence on the particular virtues that must be fostered for the proper maintenance of his ideal commonwealth. He banishes the poets, but before doing so, he anoints them with myrrh and crowns them with garlands. He must banish them on political grounds, but honours them by other standards.

Plato's discussion of poetry in *The Republic* is to be found at the end of the second and the beginning of the third Books, and in the tenth Book. In Book III he is mainly concerned with the education of the Guardians of his commonwealth, and he begins with their literary education, which he considers under three heads, theological, moral, and formal.

Now young people are impressionable, says Socrates, and 'any impression we choose to make leaves a permanent mark'. He goes on to argue that God is perfectly good, and therefore both changeless and incapable of deceit, but the poets often show him as falling short in these respects; they misrepresent gods and heroes, 'like a portrait painter who fails to catch a likeness', and thus in the theological sense they are unsuitable preceptors (*Republic* II, 377–83). On moral grounds, too, most existing poetry is unsuitable for educational purposes, for in their accounts of the gods and of the great heroes of the past the poets have depicted various forms of moral weakness, and here again they will have a bad effect on the minds of the young (ibid. III, 386–92). In the discussion of the form, or manner of presentation, of poetry we encounter for the first time the term *mimesis*, or imitation, which is to figure so largely again in Book X of *The Republic* and in Aristotle's *Poetics*. Here in Book III Plato uses it in a rather specialized sense, perhaps best translated as 'impersonation': that is, what the poet does when he is not speaking in his own person, as he does in lyric, but, by the use of direct speech in drama or in parts of epic, represents or impersonates another person. In their reading aloud from the poets (which formed a large part of Greek education) the young future Guardians, Plato causes Socrates to say, will learn by the poets' example to depart from their own characters by having to represent other characters, including bad characters. This will not do in a republic in which everyone has to learn how best to play his own part, and not to interfere with the functions of other people (ibid. III, 394–8). For his illustrations of the bad influence of the poets on the bringing up of his Guardians Plato draws chiefly on Homer, Hesiod, and the tragic playwrights.

At the beginning of Book X (595–602) Plato's general argument is that poetry and the arts are illusion. In comparison with the meaning he attaches to it in Book III, he greatly extends and deepens the sense of the term *mimesis*. He now uses it to signify imitation, or representation, in the much wider sense of the copying of reality – of the objects and circumstances of the actual world – by means of literature and the visual arts. In literature this implies the attempt to reproduce life exactly as it is. Of this Plato cannot approve, and he gives the grounds of his disapproval in terms of his Theory of Ideas. According to this theory everything that exists, or happens, in this world is an imperfect copy of an ideal object or action or state that has an ideal existence beyond this world. The productions of the poets (and artists) are therefore imitations of imperfect copies of an ideal life; they are third-hand and unreal, and can teach us nothing of value about life.

Plato goes on to argue in some detail that the appeal of poetry is to the lower, less rational, part of our nature; it strengthens the lower elements in the mind at the expense of reason.

Finally Plato takes up again the charge that poetry is a bad moral influence. But whereas in Book III he had related his argument to the education of his Guardians, here he widens its scope, as he has done with *mimesis*. He now maintains that poetry, especially dramatic poetry, has a bad moral effect on those who *hear* it, for they soon learn to admire it, and thence to model themselves on the weaknesses and faults that it represents.

This, in bare summary, is the gist of Plato's attack on poetry in *The Republic*. It may be objected that, in stressing the demoralizing effect of the worse elements in poetry, he too readily discounts the strengthening and invigorating influence that it might exert by its representation of what is good. However, he is arguing on grounds of political expediency, and, since the poet's potentialities for doing harm seem to him so great, especially by reason of the seductive charm of what he writes, he must exclude him from his ideal republic. He will allow entry to the lyrical poet who will sing in praise of the gods and of the virtues of good men, but to no other poet.

In *The Laws*, where his subject is again the nature of an ideal state, Plato's discussion of the place of literature and art in education is more general. The citizens, he says, must be educated in 'good art', and good art, he concludes, is that in which not only is the imitation – all art being imitative – as true as it is possible to make it, but also the object imitated is beautiful or good (Plato's word is *kalos*, which he uses with the sense of both 'beautiful' and 'good'). Here, then, we have at least a limited acceptance of the value of the arts. In other works, however, his disapproval is more apparent. In the *Protagoras* (326a, 339a) Protagoras voices the general current view of the poets: that since Homer they have been accepted as educators, and that their teachings help to make good citizens. In the *Lysis* (213e) they are described as 'the fathers and authors of wisdom'. But, in the arguments put forward by Socrates, Plato makes clear his belief that this indiscriminate admiration for the poets is mere superstition, and that their judgements on conduct and morality are unreliable. This unreliability comes from the fact that, as Plato expresses it in the *Apology* (22c), poets compose their works, not under the influence of wisdom, 'but by reason of some natural endowment and under the power of non-rational inspiration'. This notion of the irrationality of the poets is further developed in the *Phaedrus* (244) and the *Ion* (534), where they are equated with madmen and men who merely reproduce in a state of frenzy what the Muse has inspired them to say. Nor will Plato have anything to do with the allegorical interpretation, fashionable in his day, of that which in the poets appears obscure or contradictory. He rejects such interpretations, not only in *The Republic*, but also in the *Protagoras* (347e) and the *Phaedrus* (229).

Much has been made of Plato's animadversions on poets and poetry, but he is very far from being merely a negative critic. Even in *The Republic* (607) he is ready to give a favourable hearing to those who wish to defend poetry, 'as we shall gain much if we find her a source of profit as well as pleasure'; and, as has been shown, he is in *The Laws* prepared to accept the mimetic arts of epic and drama if only their poets will imitate worthy things.

However, he puts forward more positively constructive views than these. In the *Phaedrus* (245a, 265) he gives a deeper meaning to the concept of inspiration than that which has already been mentioned; inspiration can, indeed, give rise to the utterances of a madman, but it can also be 'a divine release of the soul from the yoke of custom and convention'. In the same work (264) he discusses the principle of organic unity, which he considers basic to the whole idea of art. He speaks to the same effect in the *Gorgias* (503), and touches on it also in *The Republic* (398). In other respects he inaugurates systems or points of view which have become commonplaces in the criticism of later ages. In *The Republic*, as has been seen, he draws distinctions, according to their manner of presentation, between epic, lyric, and drama. In *The Laws* (817) he speaks of the truest tragedy as that which represents the best and noblest type of life, a view later developed by Aristotle, and taken up by Renaissance critics. In *The Republic* (387, 605) and the *Phaedrus* (268) he accepts pity and fear as the emotions particularly awakened by tragedy, another conception which was carried further by Aristotle. In the *Philebus* (47–8) he embarks on a topic which has been much discussed by recent theorists of tragedy, that of 'tragic pleasure' – the special kind of pleasure that we derive from watching a good tragedy. He is the first critic who is known to have theorized constructively on the nature of comedy, largely in the *Philebus* (48–9). And it may be mentioned in passing that he also contributed sensibly to rhetorical theory.

So far Plato has been considered only as a speculative critic. He frequently demonstrates that he is a good practical critic as well. To give only two or three examples, in the *Symposium* (194–7) he exposes the extravagances and mannerisms of the poet Agathon by means of devastating parody. In the *Protagoras* (344) he causes Socrates to deride Protagoras and others for their misguided methods in criticizing an ode by Simonides; Socrates himself draws attention to its excellent craftsmanship and its wealth of fine detail, and says that it should be judged according to its total effect, not merely by reference to isolated phrases. Moreover, Plato more than once mocks the sensationalism of contemporary tragic playwrights, and in the *Cratylus* (425) their excessive use of the *deus ex machina* to get them out of difficult situations.

Plato is, then, an able and a very influential critic. He is not represented in the translations that appear in this volume only because *The Republic* and many of the other works which have been referred to are already available as Penguin Classics.

In a work on classical literary criticism which offers no

texts earlier than Aristotle's *Poetics* it has seemed necessary to give some account of the most significant earlier critics. Aristotle himself and Horace and Longinus may perhaps be dealt with equally briefly, since they are here to speak for themselves.

Aristotle was born at Stagira, in Macedonia, in 384 B.C. At the age of seventeen he went to Athens, where he became a pupil of Plato, at whose death twenty years later he left Athens. In 342 Philip of Macedon appointed him tutor to his young son, later Alexander the Great. On Alexander's succession to the throne in 335 Aristotle returned to Athens, and was put in charge of the Lyceum, a 'gymnasium' sacred to Apollo Lyceus. He was a man of vast erudition; his lectures and writings covered almost every aspect of human knowledge that was studied in his day, and attracted a large number of scholars to the Lyceum. After Alexander's death he was in some quarters regarded with suspicion as a friend of Alexander's, was accused of impiety, and in 322 fled to Chalcis in Euboea, where he died in the same year.

The *Poetics* cannot be dated, but it appears to be a late work by Aristotle, since it presupposes in the reader a knowledge of other mature works by Aristotle, especially the *Ethics*, the *Politics*, and the *Rhetoric* (see especially the discussion of pity and fear in *Rhetoric* II, 5, 7). The form and nature of the work have been much discussed. It is often elliptical in expression, and some of its ideas seem inadequately, at times almost incoherently, developed. These circumstances have led to a belief that it is not a treatise in anything like a final form, but consists rather of jottings or lecture-notes, whether Aristotle's own notes, or notes taken down by a pupil in a course of lectures. However, condensed as it is, it is more complete and coherent on some of the topics it treats than has always been allowed.

Aristotle opens by outlining the scope of the work – a study of the poetic kinds, that is, epic poetry, dramatic poetry, and lyrical poetry. These are the kinds that were defined by Plato, though Aristotle's later treatment of them differs from Plato's. The first three chapters are largely a discussion of imitation (*mimesis*), in Plato's later use of the word, under the heads of the objects of poetic imitation, that is, the types of men and activities that are imitated or represented, and of the manner of imitation, which, as in Plato, differentiates the three poetic kinds that have been named. The next two chapters trace the origins and development of poetry, taking in the factors that led to the differences between serious lyrical poetry and lampoon or satire, and between comedy and tragedy and epic.

In Chapter 6 Aristotle embarks upon the most important subject of the *Poetics*, tragic drama. He first describes the nature of tragedy, to which we shall return later, and its constituent parts: plot, character, diction, thought, spectacle, and song. In the following chapter he discusses the scope of the plot, and the fact that it must have a beginning, a middle, and an end, and in Chapter 8 the organic unity of the plot. Chapter 9 begins with the famous digression in which Aristotle argues that 'poetry is something more philosophical and more worthy of serious attention than history'. He goes on to draw distinctions between simple and complex plots, and to introduce us to some technical terms that played a large part both in his own and in Renaissance criticism, namely, 'reversal', 'discovery', and 'calamity'. Next he defines the main parts of tragedy, such things as the prologue, the episodes, the exode, and the choral songs. Chapters 13 and 14 contain his well-known discussion of what he means by his association of pity and fear with tragedy – a development of his definition of tragedy in Chapter 6, where in one of his most controversial phrases he spoke of their importance among the functions of tragedy: 'by means of pity and fear bringing about the purgation of such emotions'.

The next two chapters are devoted to characterization and the reasons why it is less important in tragedy than plot. Chapter 16 describes the various kinds of discovery that are appropriate to tragedy; and the following two chapters contain what might be called 'rules' for the tragic poet: the careful planning of the play, the filling in of suitable episodes, the functions of the chorus, and consideration of scope and structure. Chapter 19 concerns the elements of drama that Aristotle calls thought and diction.

Chapters 20, 21, and 22 consist largely of definitions: of

letters, syllables, and parts of speech; of figures such as metaphor; of what constitutes suitable diction.

And now at last, in the final four chapters, Aristotle gives serious consideration to epic poetry. He analyses its scope, plot, structure, and subject-matter in much the same terms as he has employed in the treatment of tragedy. And finally, having compared the two genres, finding the chief differences in the length of the work and the metre used, he comes to the conclusion that tragedy is the better of the two.

This short analysis will, I hope, have indicated the nature and range of the *Poetics*, and brought out the comparative thoroughness with which it treats at least tragedy. It will also have shown some of the differences between Aristotle's approach to poetry and Plato's. There is reason to believe that Aristotle wrote a second part, dealing with comedy, which has not survived.

The *Poetics* is often described as an answer to Plato's views on poetry. It is of course more than this, for Aristotle is much concerned with putting forward views of his own, with studying the methods of the great poets and drawing conclusions from them, and with laying down and defining a critical terminology, in doing which he rendered a valuable service to critics of later periods. Nevertheless, although he never names Plato, it is clear that he is sometimes 'answering' him. For instance, in the matter of imitation, where Plato asserts that the worth of poetry should be judged by the truth to life achieved by the imitation, not by the pleasure it gives, Aristotle argues that correct imitation is in itself a source of pleasure; and where Plato asserts that the object imitated must be beautiful, Aristotle argues that the imitation of ugly things is capable of possessing beauty. Against Plato's objection to poetry on the grounds that it excites the emotions, which ought to be kept under control, Aristotle, while agreeing that it does indeed excite the emotions, claims that in doing so it releases them, and hence has the effect of reducing them. To give one more example, Plato takes exception to poetry as an imitation of an imitation of the ideal, which places it at a considerable remove from the truth; Aristotle's answer is that, in its concern with universal truths, the poetic treatment of a subject is more valuable than a historical treatment, the aim of which is to reach the truth merely by way of facts – poetry is, indeed, more concerned with ultimate truth than history.

In a short introduction it is impossible to do more than touch on a few of the points of special interest in the *Poetics*. It is still, perhaps, necessary to begin by emphasizing that it is not a manual of instruction for the would-be playwright. Aristotle's main intention was to describe and define what appeared to have been most effective in the practice of the best poets and playwrights, and to make suggestions about what he regarded as the best procedure. The misconception, still to some extent current, that he was laying down a set of rules for composition arose with the Renaissance critics. For example, it was Castelvetro who, in his edition of the *Poetics* published in 1570, formulated in rigid terms the 'Aristotelian rules' of the three unities – the unities of time, place, and action. In fact, Aristotle only once mentions time in relation to dramatic action. In Chapter 5, speaking of differences between epic and tragedy, he says, 'Tragedy tries as far as possible to keep within a single revolution of the sun, or only slightly to exceed it, whereas the epic observes no limits in its time of action.' 'Tries as far as possible . . .': there is nothing here that can be called a rule; and indeed several of the great Attic tragedies far exceed twenty-four hours in their time of action. Nor does Aristotle lay down any rules about unity of place, or even say that it is desirable to confine the action to a single place. Certainly he insists on unity of action, and that in terms that come as close to the formulation of a rule as anything in the whole of the *Poetics*; but the doctrine of the three unities, as it has been understood in recent centuries, cannot be laid to his account.

Something must be said about the important principle of organic unity which, as we have seen, is formulated by both Plato and Aristotle, and later also by Horace and Longinus. In Chapter 7, where he is discussing some of the requirements of plot in tragedy, Aristotle says, 'Whatever is beautiful, whether it be a living creature or an object made up of various parts, must necessarily not only have its parts properly ordered, but also of an appropriate size, for beauty is bound up with size and order'; and a few lines later, 'Now in just the same way as living creatures and organisms compounded of many parts must be of a reasonable size, . . . so too plots must be of a reasonable length.' Furthermore, in Chapter 23 he declares that a well-constructed epic will be 'like a single complete organism'. As Humphry House has pointed out, the comparison of the unity of a literary work with that of a living organism is important because it refutes the charge that 'Aristotle is describing a formal, dead, mechanical kind of unity'. The notion of a living organism, when it is related to literature, implies growth and vigour in that literature, and, too, lack of uniformity, since probably no two living organisms are precisely alike.

Rather more complex is Aristotle's treatment of the relationship between plot and character in drama; but this needs to be studied in conjunction with passages of the *Ethics*, and this is not the place for such a study. Briefly, Aristotle's view is that in life character is subordinated to action because it is the product of action; it is developed in particular directions by the nature of our actions from our earliest days, and a man's bent of character can be manifested only in his actions. Similarly, in drama 'character' in its full and proper sense can be manifested only in action, and must therefore play a subordinate part to plot.

The vexed question of what Aristotle means by catharsis, or purgation, can also be fully considered only by reference to others of his writings, especially the *Rhetoric* and the *Ethics*. All that I shall say about it here is that I believe that by the catharsis of such emotions as pity and fear (Chapter 6) he means their restoration to the right proportions, to the desirable 'mean' which is the basis of his discussion of human qualities in the *Ethics*.

Two books which deal fully and helpfully with the points I have dismissed so briefly, and with others I have not mentioned, are *Aristotle's Poetics: A Course of Eight Lectures*, by Humphry House (Hart-Davis, 1956), and *Aristotle's Poetics: The Argument*, by Gerald F. Else (Harvard U.P. and O.U.P., 1957).

Horace was born at or near Venusia, in the south-east of

Italy, in 65 B.C. From his early education in Rome under the famous flogging schoolmaster Orbilius Pupillus he proceeded to Athens in order to study philosophy. While he was there Julius Caesar was assassinated, and Brutus, on his way to Macedonia, offered Horace a command in the Republican Army, which he accepted, and fought on the losing side at Philippi. Although his Italian estates were confiscated, he was allowed to return to Rome, where he served as a clerk to the treasury. Later he was introduced by his friends Virgil and Varius to Maecenas, the great patron of letters, who in the course of time became his close friend and conferred many benefits on him, including a fine estate near Tivoli. Although much courted by the Emperor Augustus, he held aloof from him for several years, but eventually gave him his warm friendship and admiration, and addressed several of his finest poems to him. Horace died in 8 B.C., a few weeks after his friend Maecenas.

One of the fruits of Horace's friendship with the Emperor is the *Epistle to Augustus* (*Epistles* II, 1). After the courtly compliments of the opening, the first ninety lines or so are an attack on those who, giving their admiration – or lip-service – to the ancients, express disapproval of contemporary literature. This attack is followed by a perceptive comparison between the origins of Greek and of Roman poetry, on much the same lines as that in the *Ars Poetica* ('Grais ingenium . . . dedit Musa'), and by an instructive outline history of Roman poetry. In line 177 Horace turns to the theatre audiences of the day, and reproves them for preferring mere spectacle to good plays and good acting. Finally he praises the Emperor's good taste, and asks him to give his patronage to other kinds of poetry than the dramatic. The epistle displays a fine independence of judgement. In the critical sense it is important for its historical retrospect; for the view it expresses that poetry should be judged by its intrinsic merits, and not for its antiquity; for its argument that the conditions in which Roman literature developed made it inevitable that it should not achieve greatness until a comparatively late period; and for its claim that such poets as Virgil and Varius were working on the right lines in their progress towards poetic immortality.

The *Epistle to Julius Florus* (*Epistles* II, 2) is to some extent autobiographical, and Horace half-playfully gives his reasons for not writing much poetry, especially lyrical poetry, at this period of his life – perhaps round about 16 or 15 B.C. For literary criticism the most important part of this poem is the section near the end in which Horace satirizes the popular but shallow poets of the day, and gives his own views on poetic technique, especially the need for the most careful revision in order to ensure that the best words have been found and set down in the best order.

Like these two works, the *Ars Poetica* is a verse epistle – *Epistula ad Pisones*; but already within a century of Horace's death Quintilian was referring to it as *Ars Poetica*, the title by which it is now generally known, or as *Liber de Arte Poetica*. The date of its composition has been a matter of dispute, but it is now widely accepted that it belongs to the end of Horace's career, to some time between 12 and 8 B.C. If this dating is correct, the father whom Horace addresses (*Piso, pater*) would probably be Lucius Piso, who was born in 50 or 49, and who was consul in 15. If this Piso had married fairly young, he could have had, in the last years of Horace's life, two sons growing towards manhood (*iuvenes*), and capable of having formed the literary ambitions which Horace attributes to the young men in the poem.

It is clear that the epistle was written primarily for the guidance of the elder son, who had in hand, or at least in mind, some literary project. The father emerges as a man of mature judgement to whom the young man may turn for advice and criticism; and the younger son figures merely as the third member of the family, no doubt also possessing literary potentialities, but too young to show any particular bent. Since so large a proportion of the poem relates to drama, it may be inferred that the elder son was engaged upon or planning some form of dramatic composition. Horace not only gives him specific advice on procedure, but also, like previous critics and like Longinus later, demonstrates that natural ability must be supplemented by careful study and guided by discipline – that literary success depends on a combination of nature and art. Furthermore, the poet must submit what he writes to rigorous criticism, and not give it to the world without the most meticulous revision.

Horace gives us in the *Ars Poetica* no strikingly profound or basically new critical doctrines. He draws freely on the Greeks and on earlier Roman writers, including Cicero. But we should not on these grounds be led to depreciate his worth as a literary critic; nor should we be deceived by his informal epistolary manner – his discursiveness, his comparative lack of method, his occasional light-heartedness. His importance lies in his consistently reasonable and practical approach to literary problems, and, it may be added, in the memorable quality that he imparts to his literary judgements.

Although the *Ars Poetica* contains no discussion of poetry as an imitative art, Horace shows an awareness of the place of imitation in its genesis. 'I would lay down,' he says, 'that the experienced poet, as an imitative artist [*doctum imitatorem*], should look to human life and character as his models, and from them derive a language that is true to life' (317–18). But just as important to him is the inventiveness which produces fictions designed to give pleasure (388). He makes more of the aims and functions of poetry, and the terms in which he does so illustrate the memorable quality of his utterance to which I referred in the last paragraph:

> aut prodesse volunt aut delectare poetae,
> aut simul et iucunda et idonea dicere vitae (333–4).

'Poets aim at giving either profit or delight, or at combining the giving of pleasure with some useful precepts for life.' And a few lines later:

> omne tulit punctum qui miscuit utile dulci,
> lectorem delectando pariterque monendo (343–4).

'The man who has managed to blend profit with delight wins everyone's approbation, for he gives his reader pleasure at the same time as he instructs him.' This doctrine was endlessly echoed and developed by Renaissance critics.

Horace also has strong views on another function of poetry, the power it possesses, or at least has manifested in the past, of advancing civilization. The clearest expression of this view is found in lines 391–407; and there is a parallel in lines 126–38 of the *Epistle to Augustus.*

Cicero had advocated the imitation of ancient models, as Longinus was also to do later, but Horace was the first critic to lay down this doctrine with regard to poetry. 'You must give your days and nights to the study of Greek models,' he says (268–9); and his mentioning only Homer and the Attic tragic playwrights makes it clear that he is thinking especially of the great writers of the classical period of Greek literature. This doctrine of imitation of the ancients was also much canvassed at the Renaissance. Other topics on which Horace lays emphasis are the need for organic unity, which had already been stressed by Plato and Aristotle; the need for sound and appropriate subject-matter; and the correct choice of diction and metre.

All these points may be applied to poetry generally. What Horace says specifically about drama and its techniques, although it takes up a large part of the epistle, seems clear enough, and is to some extent familiar from Aristotle; it needs no analysis here.

However, one further matter demands attention, and this is the principle of decorum, which is fundamental to Horace's literary theory, and which is touched on at intervals throughout the *Ars Poetica.* This doctrine of fitness, or literary propriety, had been discussed by Aristotle, and Cicero made much of it in his rhetorical theory, especially in the *De Oratore*; but for Horace it constitutes, in the words of J. W. H. Atkins, 'a guiding and dominating principle'. Horace applies it here particularly to poetry, and especially dramatic poetry. Every part and every aspect of the work must be appropriate to the nature of the work as a whole: the choice of subject in relation to the chosen genre, the characterization, the form, the expression, the metre, the style, and tone; the poet must avoid the mixing of genres, the creation of characters who lack verisimilitude, the excessive or improper use of the *deus ex machina.* Nor should anything revolting or unnatural be enacted on the stage:

> ne pueros coram populo Medea trucidet . . . (185)

'Medea must not butcher her children in the presence of the audience ...'. The principle of decorum is yet another of Horace's doctrines which pervade the literary criticism of the Renaissance.

Of Horace and his career we know much. Of the author of the famous treatise *On the Sublime* nothing is known, not even his name. The nature and treatment of the subject-matter of this work suggest that it was written in the first century A.D., partly as a corrective to a lost work on the same subject by a certain Cecilius, who was a friend of Dionysius of Halicarnassus. It may have been by false association in later times with Dionysius, and by a similar error with regard to a third-century critic named Cassius Longinus, that the oldest manuscript, the tenth-century Paris manuscript, attributes the treatise to 'Dionysius *or* Longinus'. In view of the centuries-long tradition, and the awkwardness of such terms as 'the pseudo-Longinus' or 'the treatise attributed to Longinus', I am retaining the name Longinus. Of the Terentianus who is repeatedly addressed as the recipient of the work (in the very first sentence he is, in the Paris manuscript, for some unknown reason named as Postumius Florentianus) nothing is certainly known. The authorship of the treatise and the identity of Terentianus are fully discussed in Roberts's introduction to the edition which I later name as my copy text, and in Chapter VI of J. W. H. Atkins's *Literary Criticism in Antiquity*, Volume II. It should be added that the treatise as we have it is unfinished, and that it is also marred by half a dozen lacunae amounting to the loss of twenty pages, or perhaps a thousand lines. Grievous as these losses are, the considerably larger quantity that remains is complete and coherent enough to leave us with a critical work of very great interest and value.

I have also followed tradition in translating the key-word of the treatise, *ὕψος* (*hypsos*), as sublimity. However, the word does not, as Longinus uses it, mean precisely what we associate today with sublimity, that is, an outstanding and unusual exaltation of conception and style. As Longinus defines it, it signifies a certain distinction and excellence of expression, that distinction and excellence by which authors have been enabled to win immortal fame. There appears to be no single English word which fully conveys all this, but if Longinus's initial definition is kept in mind, the meaning of 'sublimity' in the translation should always be clear. I have reserved such possible alternatives as 'grandeur' and 'the Grand Style' for occasions on which Longinus uses compounds of the word μέγας ('great').

Although he occasionally digresses, Longinus never loses sight of his subject – the qualities and devices that make for, or militate against, the production of the sublime. Having defined the term, he asks whether there is such a thing as an art of the sublime. His answer recalls what we have already heard from Horace and other earlier critics: sublimity, he says, is innate, an inborn gift, but it must be cultivated, among other ways by imitation or emulation of writers who have shown themselves capable of achieving sublimity; art is necessary if the natural ability is to be used to the best effect. Longinus does not expect that any writer should maintain an unbroken level of sublimity; even the godlike Homer and Plato have their lapses, and many other writers cannot long sustain the sublimity to which they are capable of rising. However, the writer who can occasionally flash into sublimity is superior to the one who, like Hyperides, does everything well, but never quite achieves the sublime.

The main body of the treatise is concerned with the discussion and illustration of five sources of the sublime. The first and most important source (Chapters 8–15) is grandeur of thought, the ability to form grand conceptions. This takes its rise in nobility of soul or character, and Longinus illustrates it from Homer and from the Book of Genesis. It may also result from the right choice and arrangement of the most striking circumstances, as he illustrates by a perceptive analysis of an ode by Sappho. After some consideration of imagery, Longinus speaks of the second source, that is, vehement and inspired passion; however, he does not develop this, but promises to deal with it in a separate work.

The third source of the sublime is the effective use of stylistic and rhetorical figures (Chapters 16–29); and Longinus observes that a figure is best used when the fact that it is a figure escapes attention. The fourth source is to be found in noble diction and phrasing (Chapters 30–8); this includes the skilful use of metaphors and other figures of speech. Finally (Chapters 39–40) comes dignified and elevated composition, that is, an insistence on the most effective arrangement of words, and the now well established conception of organic unity.

Longinus's concreteness adds considerably to the value of his criticism. He keeps it concrete by means of constant illustration and analysis, often very shrewd analysis. His reference to the lawgiver of the Jews and his pronouncement at the beginning of his *Laws*, 'God said . . . Let there be light, and there was light; let there be land, and there was land,' is of particular interest, and has led to much speculation about the currency of the Hebrew scriptures in Longinus's time; however, it seems profitless to speculate whether Longinus supplied it from an imperfect memory of what he had himself read in the Septuagint, whether he derived it from his reading of Cecilius or of some other writer, or whether it is an interpolation belonging to a later period. There it stands among the many quotations which establish Longinus as a fine judicial, as well as speculative, critic. One remembers also his sensible analyses of many passages of Homer and Plato and Demosthenes, his admirable comments on the ode of Sappho which he quotes, and his telling comparisons between Demosthenes and Cicero and Demosthenes and Hyperides. He must be ranked as one of the finest and most constructive of the classical literary critics.

A large and important branch of classical criticism is that which relates to rhetorical theory. This has necessarily been excluded from the present work, since it would have opened up a field too vast to be treated in a single volume with the authors here represented.

The texts I have used for the translations in this volume are as follows: for Aristotle the text of Ingram Bywater in the Oxford Classical Texts; for Horace that of E. C. Wickham, revised by H. W. Garrod, in the same series; for Longinus the Cambridge edition, with introduction and translation, of

W. Rhys Roberts. For their generous help, both in the solution of difficulties and in matters of expression, my gratitude is due to my colleague at Westfield College, Miss Christina Barratt, to the late General Editor of the Penguin Classics, Dr E. V. Rieu, and to the present Joint Editor, Mrs Radice.

ARISTOTLE

On the Art of Poetry

ARISTOTLE
On the Art of Poetry

INTRODUCTION

Poetry as Imitation

UNDER the general heading of the art of poetry, I propose not only to speak about this art itself, but also to discuss the various kinds of poetry and their characteristic functions, the types of plot-structure that are required if a poem is to succeed, the number and nature of its constituent parts, and similarly any other matters that may be relevant to a study of this kind. I shall begin in the natural way, that is, by going back to first principles.

Epic and tragic poetry, comedy too, dithyrambic poetry, and most music composed for the flute and the lyre, can all be described in general terms as forms of imitation or representation. However, they differ from one another in three respects: either in using different media for the representation, or in representing different things, or in representing them in entirely different ways.

CHAPTER I

The Media of Poetic Imitation

SOME artists, whether by theoretical knowledge or by long practice, can represent things by imitating their shapes and colours, and others do so by the use of the voice; in the arts I have spoken of the imitation is produced by means of rhythm, language, and music, these being used either separately or in combination. Thus the art of the flute and of the lyre consists only in music and rhythm, as does any other of the same type, such as that of the pipes. The imitative medium of dancers is rhythm alone, unsupported by music, for it is by the manner in which they arrange the rhythms of their movements that they represent men's characters and feelings and actions.

The form of art that uses language alone, whether in prose or verse, and verse either in a mixture of metres or in one particular kind, has up to the present been without a name. For we have no common name that we can apply to the prose mimes of Sophron and Xenarchus and the Socratic dialogues, or to compositions employing iambic trimeters or elegiac couplets or any other metres of these types. We can say only that people associate poetry with the metre employed, and speak, for example, of elegiac poets and epic poets; they call them poets, however, not from the fact that they are making imitations, but indiscriminately from the fact that they are writing in metre. For it is customary to describe as poets even those who produce medical and scientific works in verse. Yet Homer and Empedocles have nothing in common except their metre, and therefore, while it is right to call the one a poet, the other should rather be called a natural philosopher than a poet. In the same way, an author composing his imitation in a mixture of all the metres, as Chaeremon did in his *Centaur*, a rhapsody employing just such a mixture, would also have to be called a poet. Such are the distinctions I would make.

Again, there are some arts which make use of all the media I have mentioned, that is, rhythm, music, and formal metre;

such are dithyrambic and nomic poetry,[1] tragedy and comedy. They differ, however, in that the first two use all these media together, while the last two use them separately, one after another.

These, then, are what I mean by the differences between the arts as far as the media of representation are concerned.

CHAPTER 2

The Objects of Poetic Imitation

SINCE imitative artists represent men in action, and men who are necessarily either of good or of bad character (for as all people differ in their moral nature according to the degree of their goodness or badness, characters almost always fall into one or other of these types), these men must be represented either as better than we are, or worse, or as the same kind of people as ourselves. Thus among the painters Polygnotus represented his subjects as better, and Pauson as worse, while Dionysius painted them just as they were. It is clear that each of the kinds of imitation I have referred to will admit of these variations, and they will differ in this way according to the differences in the objects they represent. Such diversities may occur even in dancing, and in music for the flute and the lyre; they occur also in the art that is based on language, whether it uses prose or verse unaccompanied by music. Homer, for example, depicts the better types of men, and Cleophon normal types, while Hegemon of Thasos, the first writer of parodies, and Nicochares, the author of the *Deiliad*, show them in a bad light. The same thing happens in dithyrambic and nomic poetry; for instance, the Cyclops might be represented in different ways, as was done by Timotheus and Philoxenus. This is the difference that marks the distinction between comedy and tragedy; for comedy aims at representing men as worse than they are nowadays, tragedy as better.

1. The Nome, or nomic song, was an ancient type of ode, akin to the dithyramb, sung to the lyre or flute in honour of some god, usually Apollo.

CHAPTER 3

The Manner of Poetic Imitation

THERE remains the third point of difference in these arts, that is, the manner in which each kind of subject may be represented. For it is possible, using the same medium, to represent the same subjects in a variety of ways. It may be done partly by narration and partly by the assumption of a character other than one's own, which is Homer's way; or by speaking in one's own person without any such change; or by representing the characters as performing all the actions dramatically.

These, then, as I pointed out at the beginning, are the three factors by which the imitative arts are differentiated: their media, the objects they represent, and their manner of representation. Thus in one sense Sophocles might be called an imitator of the same kind as Homer, for they both represent good men; in another sense he is like Aristophanes, in that they both represent men in action, men actually doing things. And this, some say, is why their works are called dramas, from their representing men doing things.[1] For this reason too the Dorians claim the invention of both tragedy and comedy. Comedy is claimed by the Megarians, both by those here in Greece on the grounds that it came into being when they became a democracy, and by those in Sicily because the poet Epicharmus, who was much earlier than Chionides and Magnes, came from there; certain Dorians of the Peloponnese lay claim also to tragedy. They regard the names as proof of their belief, pointing out that, whereas the Athenians call outlying villages δῆμοι (*dēmoi*), they themselves call them κῶμαι (*kōmai*); so that comedians take their name, not from κωμάζειν (*kōmazein*, 'to revel'), but from their touring in the κῶμαι when lack of appreciation drove them from the city. Furthermore, their

1. The word 'drama' means literally 'a thing done', and is derived from the verb δρᾶν (*drān*, 'to do') which here provides the translation 'doing things'. Cf. the last sentence of the paragraph.

word for 'to do' is δρᾶν (*drān*), whereas the Athenian word is πράττειν (*prattein*).

So much then for the number and character of the different kinds of imitation.

CHAPTER 4

The Origins and Development of Poetry

THE creation of poetry generally is due to two causes, both rooted in human nature. The instinct for imitation is inherent in man from his earliest days; he differs from other animals in that he is the most imitative of creatures, and he learns his earliest lessons by imitation. Also inborn in all of us is the instinct to enjoy works of imitation. What happens in actual experience is evidence of this; for we enjoy looking at the most accurate representations of things which in themselves we find painful to see, such as the forms of the lowest animals and of corpses. The reason for this is that learning is a very great pleasure, not for philosophers only, but for other people as well, however limited their capacity for it may be. They enjoy seeing likenesses because in doing so they acquire information (they reason out what each represents, and discover, for instance, that 'this is a picture of so and so'); for if by any chance the thing depicted has not been seen before, it will not be the fact that it is an imitation of something that gives the pleasure, but the execution or the colouring or some other such cause.

The instinct for imitation, then, is natural to us, as is also a feeling for music and for rhythm – and metres are obviously detached sections of rhythms. Starting from these natural aptitudes, and by a series of for the most part gradual improvements on their first efforts, men eventually created poetry from their improvisations.

However, poetry soon branched into two channels, according to the temperaments of individual poets. The more serious-minded among them represented noble actions and the doings of noble persons, while the more trivial wrote about the meaner sort of people; thus while the one type wrote hymns and panegyrics, these others began by writing invectives. We know of no poems of this kind by any poet earlier than Homer, though it is likely enough that many poets wrote them; but from Homer onwards examples may be found, his own *Margites*, for instance, and poems of the same type. It was in such poems that the iambic metre was brought into use because of its appropriateness for the purpose, and it is still called iambic today, from being the metre in which they wrote 'iambs', or lampoons, against one another.

In this way it came about that some of our early poets became writers of heroic, and some of iambic verse. But just as Homer was the supreme poet in the serious style, standing alone both in excellence of composition and in the dramatic quality of his representations of life, so also, in the dramatic character that he imparted, not to invective, but to his treatment of the ridiculous, he was the first to indicate the forms that comedy was to assume; for his *Margites* bears the same relationship to our comedies as his *Iliad* and *Odyssey* bear to our tragedies. When tragedy and comedy appeared, those whose natural aptitude inclined them towards the one kind of poetry wrote comedies instead of lampoons, and those who were drawn to the other wrote tragedies instead of epics; for these new forms were both grander and more highly regarded than the earlier.

It is beyond my scope here to consider whether or not tragedy is now developed as far as it can be in its various forms, and to decide this both absolutely and in relation to the stage.

Both tragedy and comedy had their first beginnings in improvisation. The one originated with those who led the dithyramb, the other with the leaders of the phallic songs which still survive today as traditional institutions in many of our cities. Little by little tragedy advanced, each new element being developed as it came into use, until after many changes it attained its natural form and came to a standstill. Aeschylus was the first to increase the number of actors from one to two, cut down the role of the chorus, and give the first place to the dialogue. Sophocles introduced three actors and painted scenery. As for the grandeur of tragedy, it was not until late that it acquired its characteristic stateliness, when, progressing beyond the methods of satyric drama,[1] it discarded slight plots and comic diction, and its metre changed from the trochaic tetrameter to the iambic. At first the poets had used the tetrameter because they were writing satyr-poetry, which was more closely related to the dance; but once dialogue had been introduced, by its very nature it hit upon the right measure, for the iambic is of all measures the one best suited to speech. This is shown by the fact that we most usually drop into iambics in our conversation with one another, whereas we seldom talk in hexameters, and then only when we depart from the normal tone of conversation. Another change was the increased number of episodes, or acts. We must pass over such other matters as the various embellishments of tragedy and the circumstances in which they are said to have been introduced, for it would probably be a long business to go into them in any detail.

CHAPTER 5

The Rise of Comedy. Epic Compared with Tragedy

As I have remarked, comedy represents the worse types of men; worse, however, not in the sense that it embraces any and every kind of badness, but in the sense that the ridiculous is a species of ugliness or badness. For the ridiculous consists in some form of error or ugliness that is not painful or injurious; the comic mask, for example, is distorted and ugly, but causes no pain.

Now we know something of the successive stages by which tragedy developed, and of those who were responsible for them; the early history of comedy, however, is obscure, because it was not taken seriously. It was a long time before the archon granted a chorus to comedies; until then the performers were volunteers.[2] Comedy had already acquired

1. Satyric drama is described on p. 86–7, footnote 3.
2. The Greek dramatist submitted his play to the archon, or magistrate,

certain clear-cut forms before there is any mention of those who are named as its poets. Nor is it known who introduced masks, or prologues, or a plurality of actors, and other things of that kind. Properly worked out plots originated in Sicily with Epicharmus and Phormis; of Athenian poets Crates was the first to discard the lampoon pattern and to adopt stories and plots of a more general nature.

Epic poetry agrees with tragedy to the extent that it is a representation, in dignified verse, of serious actions. They differ, however, in that epic keeps to a single metre and is in narrative form. Another point of difference is their length: tragedy tries as far as possible to keep within a single revolution of the sun, or only slightly to exceed it, whereas the epic observes no limits in its time of action – although at first the practice in this respect was the same in tragedies as in epics. Of the constituent parts, some are common to both kinds, and some are peculiar to tragedy. Thus anyone who can discriminate between what is good and what is bad in tragedy can do the same with epic; for all the elements of epic are found in tragedy, though not everything that belongs to tragedy is to be found in epic.[1]

CHAPTER 6

A Description of Tragedy

I SHALL speak later about the form of imitation that uses hexameters and about comedy, but for the moment I propose to discuss tragedy, first drawing together the definition of its essential character from what has already been said.

Tragedy, then, is a representation of an action that is worth

1. Herein, it is perhaps worth pointing out, lies the justification of the far fuller treatment that Aristotle gives to drama.

---

in charge of the religious festival at which he hoped to have it performed. If the play was chosen for performance, the archon 'granted it a chorus'; that is, he provided a choregus, a wealthy citizen who, as a form of public service, paid the expenses of the production. The earlier 'volunteers' presumably paid their own expenses.

serious attention, complete in itself, and of some amplitude; in language enriched by a variety of artistic devices appropriate to the several parts of the play; presented in the form of action, not narration; by means of pity and fear bringing about the purgation of such emotions. By language that is enriched I refer to language possessing rhythm, and music or song; and by artistic devices appropriate to the several parts I mean that some are produced by the medium of verse alone, and others again with the help of song.

Now since the representation is carried out by men performing the actions, it follows, in the first place, that spectacle is an essential part of tragedy, and secondly that there must be song and diction, these being the medium of representation. By diction I mean here the arrangement of the verses; song is a term whose sense is obvious to everyone.

In tragedy it is action that is imitated, and this action is brought about by agents who necessarily display certain distinctive qualities both of character and of thought, according to which we also define the nature of the actions. Thought and character are, then, the two natural causes of actions, and it is on them that all men depend for success or failure. The representation of the action is the plot of the tragedy; for the ordered arrangement of the incidents is what I mean by plot. Character, on the other hand, is that which enables us to define the nature of the participants, and thought comes out in what they say when they are proving a point or expressing an opinion.

Necessarily, then, every tragedy has six constituents, which will determine its quality. They are plot, character, diction, thought, spectacle, and song. Of these, two represent the media in which the action is represented, one involves the manner of representation, and three are connected with the objects of the representation; beyond them nothing further is required. These, it may be said, are the dramatic elements that have been used by practically all playwrights; for all plays alike possess spectacle, character, plot, diction, song, and thought.

Of these elements the most important is the plot, the ordering of the incidents; for tragedy is a representation, not of men, but of action and life, of happiness and unhappiness – and happiness and unhappiness are bound up with action. The purpose of living is an end which is a kind of activity, not a quality; it is their characters, indeed, that make men what they are, but it is by reason of their actions that they are happy or the reverse. Tragedies are not performed, therefore, in order to represent character, although character is involved for the sake of the action. Thus the incidents and the plot are the end aimed at in tragedy, and as always, the end is everything. Furthermore, there could not be a tragedy without action, but there could be without character; indeed the tragedies of most of our recent playwrights fail to present character, and the same might be said of many playwrights of other periods. A similar contrast could be drawn between Zeuxis and Polygnotus as painters, for Polygnotus represents character well, whereas Zeuxis is not concerned with it in his painting. Again, if someone writes a series of speeches expressive of character, and well composed as far as thought and diction are concerned, he will still not achieve the proper effect of tragedy; this will be done much better by a tragedy which is less successful in its use of these elements, but which has a plot giving an ordered combination of incidents. Another point to note is that the two most important means by which tragedy plays on our feelings, that is, 'reversals' and 'recognitions', are both constituents of the plot. A further proof is that beginners can achieve accuracy in diction and the portrayal of character before they can construct a plot out of the incidents, and this could be said of almost all the earliest dramatic poets.

The plot, then, is the first essential of tragedy, its life-blood, so to speak, and character takes the second place. It is much the same in painting; for if an artist were to daub his canvas with the most beautiful colours laid on at random, he would not give the same pleasure as he would by drawing a recognizable portrait in black and white. Tragedy is the representation of an action, and it is chiefly on account of the action that it is also a representation of persons.

The third property of tragedy is thought. This is the ability to say what is possible and appropriate in any given circumstances; it is what, in the speeches in the play, is related to the arts of politics and rhetoric. The older dramatic poets made their characters talk like statesmen, whereas those of today make them talk like rhetoricians. Character is that which reveals personal choice, the kinds of thing a man chooses or rejects when that is not obvious. Thus there is no revelation of character in speeches in which the speaker shows no preferences or aversions whatever. Thought, on the other hand, is present in speeches where something is being shown to be true or untrue, or where some general opinion is being expressed.

Fourth comes the diction of the speeches. By diction I mean, as I have already explained, the expressive use of words, and this has the same force in verse and in prose.

Of the remaining elements, the music is the most important of the pleasurable additions to the play. Spectacle, or stage-effect, is an attraction, of course, but it has the least to do with the playwright's craft or with the art of poetry. For the power of tragedy is independent both of performance and of actors, and besides, the production of spectacular effects is more the province of the property-man than of the playwright.

CHAPTER 7

The Scope of the Plot

NOW that these definitions have been established, I must go on to discuss the arrangement of the incidents, for this is of the first importance in tragedy. I have already laid down that tragedy is the representation of an action that is complete and whole and of a certain amplitude – for a thing may be whole and yet lack amplitude. Now a whole is that which has a beginning, a middle, and an end. A beginning is that which does not necessarily come after something else, although something else exists or comes about after it. An end, on the contrary, is that which naturally follows something else either as a necessary or as a usual consequence, and is not itself followed by anything. A middle is that which follows something else, and is itself followed by something. Thus well-constructed plots must neither begin nor end in a haphazard way, but must conform to the pattern I have been describing.

Furthermore, whatever is beautiful, whether it be a living creature or an object made up of various parts, must necessarily not only have its parts properly ordered, but also be of an appropriate size, for beauty is bound up with size and order. A minutely small creature, therefore, would not be beautiful, for it would take almost no time to see it and our perception of it would be blurred; nor would an extremely large one, for it could not be taken in all at once, and its unity and wholeness would be lost to the view of the beholder – if, for example, there were a creature a thousand miles long.

Now in just the same way as living creatures and organisms compounded of many parts must be of a reasonable size, so that they can be easily taken in by the eye, so too plots must be of a reasonable length, so that they may be easily held in the memory. The limits in length to be observed, in as far as they concern performance on the stage, have nothing to do with dramatic art; for if a hundred tragedies had to be performed in the dramatic contests, they would be regulated in length by the water-clock, as indeed it is said they were at one time.[1] With regard to the limit set by the nature of the action, the longer the story is the more beautiful it will be, provided that it is quite clear. To give a simple definition, a length which, as a matter either of probability or of necessity, allows of a change from misery to happiness or from happiness to misery is the proper limit of length to be observed.

CHAPTER 8

Unity of Plot

A PLOT does not possess unity, as some people suppose, merely because it is about one man. Many things, countless things indeed, may happen to one man, and some of them will not contribute to any kind of unity; and similarly he may

1. There is no evidence elsewhere that this was ever done, and it seems an improbable proceeding. One is almost tempted to accept Schmidt's emendation (εἰώθασιν for φασιν) and translate, 'as is regularly done at certain other times', i.e., with pleas in the law-courts.

carry out many actions from which no single unified action will emerge. It seems, therefore, that all those poets have been on the wrong track who have written a *Heracleid*, or a *Theseid*, or some other poem of this kind, in the belief that, Heracles being a single person, his story must necessarily possess unity. Homer, exceptional in this as in all other respects, seems, whether by art or by instinct, to have been well aware of what was required. In writing his *Odyssey* he did not put in everything that happened to Odysseus, that he was wounded on Mount Parnassus, for example, or that he feigned madness at the time of the call to arms, for it was not a matter of necessity or probability that either of these incidents should have led to the other; on the contrary, he constructed the *Odyssey* round a single action of the kind I have spoken of, and he did this with the *Iliad* too. Thus, just as in the other imitative arts each individual representation is the representation of a single object, so too the plot of a play, being the representation of an action, must present it as a unified whole; and its various incidents must be so arranged that if any one of them is differently placed or taken away the effect of wholeness will be seriously disrupted. For if the presence or absence of something makes no apparent difference, it is no real part of the whole.

CHAPTER 9

Poetic Truth and Historical Truth

IT will be clear from what I have said that it is not the poet's function to describe what has actually happened, but the kinds of thing that might happen, that is, that could happen because they are, in the circumstances, either probable or necessary. The difference between the historian and the poet is not that the one writes in prose and the other in verse; the work of Herodotus might be put into verse, and in this metrical form it would be no less a kind of history than it is without metre. The difference is that the one tells of what has happened, the other of the kinds of things that might happen. For this reason poetry is something more philosophical and more worthy of serious attention than history; for while poetry is concerned with universal truths, history treats of particular facts.

By universal truths are to be understood the kinds of thing a certain type of person will probably or necessarily say or do in a given situation; and this is the aim of poetry, although it gives individual names to its characters. The particular facts of the historian are what, say, Alcibiades did, or what happened to him. By now this distinction has become clear where comedy is concerned, for comic poets build up their plots out of probable occurrences, and then add any names that occur to them; they do not, like the iambic poets, write about actual people.[1] In tragedy, on the other hand, the authors keep to the names of real people, the reason being that what is possible is credible. Whereas we cannot be certain of the possibility of something that has not happened, what has happened is obviously possible, for it would not have happened if this had not been so. Nevertheless, even in some tragedies only one or two of the names are well known, and the rest are fictitious; and indeed there are some in which nothing is familiar, Agathon's *Antheus*, for example, in which both the incidents and the names are fictitious, and the play is none the less well liked for that. It is not necessary, therefore, to keep entirely to the traditional stories which form the subjects of our tragedies. Indeed it would be absurd to do so, since even the familiar stories are familiar only to a few, and yet they please everybody.

What I have said makes it obvious that the poet must be a maker of plots rather than of verses, since he is a poet by virtue of his representation, and what he represents is actions. And even if he writes about things that have actually happened, that does not make him any the less a poet, for there is nothing to prevent some of the things that have happened from being in accordance with the laws of possibility and probability, and thus he will be a poet in writing about them.

1. The old iambic or lampooning poets, of whom the earliest and greatest was Archilochus (seventh century B.C.), wrote about real people, as did the poets of the Old Comedy, such as Aristophanes. In the New Comedy, of which Menander is the greatest representative, the names were stock names which, though they might sometimes by association or etymology have a certain appropriateness, were not those of real people.

Of simple plots and actions those that are episodic are the worst. By an episodic plot I mean one in which the sequence of the episodes is neither probable nor necessary. Plays of this kind are written by bad poets because they cannot help it, and by good poets because of the actors; writing for the dramatic competitions, they often strain a plot beyond the bounds of possibility, and are thus obliged to dislocate the continuity of events.

However, tragedy is the representation not only of a complete action, but also of incidents that awaken fear and pity, and effects of this kind are heightened when things happen unexpectedly as well as logically, for then they will be more remarkable than if they seem merely mechanical or accidental. Indeed, even chance occurrences seem most remarkable when they have the appearance of having been brought about by design – when, for example, the statue of Mitys at Argos killed the man who had caused Mitys's death by falling down on him at a public entertainment. Things like this do not seem mere chance occurrences. Thus plots of this type are necessarily better than others.

CHAPTER 10

Simple and Complex Plots

SOME plots are simple, and some complex, for the obvious reason that the actions of which they are representations are of one or other of these kinds. By a simple action I refer to one which is single and continuous in the sense of my earlier definition, and in which the change of fortune comes about without a reversal or a discovery. A complex action is one in which the change is accompanied by a discovery or a reversal, or both. These should develop out of the very structure of the plot, so that they are the inevitable or probable consequence of what has gone before, for there is a big difference between what happens as a result of something else and what merely happens after it.

CHAPTER II

Reversal, Discovery, and Calamity

As has already been noted, a reversal is a change from one state of affairs to its opposite, one which conforms, as I have said, to probability or necessity. In *Oedipus*, for example, the Messenger who came to cheer Oedipus and relieve him of his fear about his mother did the very opposite by revealing to him who he was. In the *Lynceus*, again, Lynceus is being led off to execution, followed by Danaus who is to kill him, when, as a result of events that occurred earlier, it comes about that he is saved and it is Danaus who is put to death.

As the word itself indicates, a discovery is a change from ignorance to knowledge, and it leads either to love or to hatred between persons destined for good or ill fortune. The most effective form of discovery is that which is accompanied by reversals, like the one in *Oedipus*. There are of course other forms of discovery, for what I have described may happen in relation to inanimate and trifling objects, and moreover it is possible to discover whether a person has done something or not. But the form of discovery most essentially related to the plot and action of the play is the one described above, for a discovery of this kind in combination with a reversal will carry with it either pity or fear, and it is such actions as these that, according to my definition, tragedy represents; and further, such a combination is likely to lead to a happy or an unhappy ending.

As it is persons who are involved in the discovery, it may be that only one person's identity is revealed to another, that of the second being already known. Sometimes, however, a natural recognition of two parties is necessary, as for example, when the identity of Iphigenia was made known to Orestes by the sending of the letter, and a second discovery was required to make him known to Iphigenia.

Two elements of plot, then, reversal and discovery, turn upon such incidents as these. A third is suffering, or calamity.

Of these three, reversal and discovery have already been defined. A calamity is an action of a destructive or painful nature, such as death openly represented, excessive suffering, wounding, and the like.

CHAPTER 12

The Main Parts of Tragedy

I SPOKE earlier of the various elements that are to be employed as the constituents of tragedy. The separate sections into which the work is divided are as follows: prologue, episode, exode, and choral song, the last being subdivided into parode and stasimon. These are common to all tragedies; songs from the actors and 'commoi', however, are a characteristic only of some tragedies.

The prologue is the whole of that part of a tragedy that precedes the parode, or first entry of the Chorus. An episode is the whole of that part of a tragedy that comes between complete choral songs. The exode is the whole of that part of a tragedy which is not followed by a song of the Chorus. In the choral sections the parode is the whole of the first utterance of the Chorus, and a stasimon is a choral song without anapaests or trochees. A 'commos' is a passage of lament in which both Chorus and actors take part.

These then are the separate sections into which the body of the tragedy is to be divided; I mentioned earlier the elements of which it must be composed.

CHAPTER 13

Tragic Action

FOLLOWING upon the points I have already made, I must go on to say what is to be aimed at and what guarded against in the construction of plots, and what are the sources of the tragic effect.

We saw that the structure of tragedy at its best should be complex, not simple, and that it should represent actions capable of awakening fear and pity – for this is a characteristic function of representations of this type. It follows in the first place that good men should not be shown passing from prosperity to misery, for this does not inspire fear or pity, it merely disgusts us. Nor should evil men be shown progressing from misery to prosperity. This is the most untragic of all plots, for it has none of the requisites of tragedy; it does not appeal to our humanity, or awaken pity or fear in us. Nor again should an utterly worthless man be seen falling from prosperity into misery. Such a course might indeed play upon our humane feelings, but it would not arouse either pity or fear; for our pity is awakened by undeserved misfortune, and our fear by that of someone just like ourselves – pity for the undeserving sufferer and fear for the man like ourselves – so that the situation in question would have nothing in it either pitiful or fearful.

There remains a mean between these extremes. This is the sort of man who is not conspicuous for virtue and justice, and whose fall into misery is not due to vice and depravity, but rather to some error, a man who enjoys prosperity and a high reputation, like Oedipus and Thyestes and other famous members of families like theirs.

Inevitably, then, the well-conceived plot will have a single interest, and not, as some say, a double. The change in fortune will be, not from misery to prosperity, but the reverse, from prosperity to misery, and it will be due, not to depravity, but to some great error either in such a man as I have described or in one better than this, but not worse. This is borne out by existing practice. For at first the poets treated any stories that came to hand, but nowadays the best tragedies are written about a handful of families, those of Alcmaeon, for example, and Oedipus and Orestes and Meleager and Thyestes and Telephus, and others whom it has befallen to suffer or inflict terrible experiences.

The best tragedies in the technical sense are constructed in this way. Those critics are on the wrong tack, therefore, who criticize Euripides for following such a procedure in his tragedies, and complain that many of them end in misfortune;

for, as I have said, this is the right ending. The strongest evidence of this is that on the stage and in the dramatic competitions plays of this kind, when properly worked out, are the most tragic of all, and Euripides, faulty as is his management of other points, is nevertheless regarded as the most tragic of our dramatic poets.

The next best type of structure, ranked first by some critics, is that which, like the *Odyssey*, has a double thread of plot, and ends in opposite ways for the good and the bad characters. It is considered the best only because of the feeble judgement of the audience, for the poets pander to the taste of the spectators. But this is not the pleasure that is proper to tragedy. It belongs rather to comedy, where those who have been the bitterest of enemies in the original story, Orestes and Aegisthus, for example, go off at the end as friends, and nobody is killed by anybody.

CHAPTER 14

Fear and Pity

FEAR and pity may be excited by means of spectacle; but they can also take their rise from the very structure of the action, which is the preferable method and the mark of a better dramatic poet. For the plot should be so ordered that even without seeing it performed anyone merely hearing what is afoot will shudder with fear and pity as a result of what is happening – as indeed would be the experience of anyone hearing the story of Oedipus. To produce this effect by means of stage-spectacle is less artistic, and requires the cooperation of the producer. Those who employ spectacle to produce an effect, not of fear, but of something merely monstrous, have nothing to do with tragedy, for not every kind of pleasure should be demanded of tragedy, but only that which is proper to it; and since the dramatic poet has by means of his representation to produce the tragic pleasure that is associated with pity and fear, it is obvious that this effect is bound up with the events of the plot.

Let us now consider what kinds of incident are to be

regarded as fearful or pitiable. Deeds that fit this description must of course involve people who are either friends to one another, or enemies, or neither. Now if a man injures his enemy, there is nothing pitiable either in his act or in his intention, except in so far as suffering is inflicted; nor is there if they are indifferent to each other. But when the sufferings involve those who are near and dear to one another, when for example brother kills brother, son father, mother son, or son mother, or if such a deed is contemplated, or something else of the kind is actually done, then we have a situation of the kind to be aimed at. Thus it will not do to tamper with the traditional stories, the murder of Clytemnestra by Orestes, for instance, and that of Eriphyle by Alcmaeon; on the other hand, the poet must use his imagination and handle the traditional material effectively.

I must explain more clearly what I mean by 'effectively'. The deed may be done by characters acting consciously and in full knowledge of the facts, as was the way of the early dramatic poets, when for instance Euripides made Medea kill her children. Or they may do it without realizing the horror of the deed until later, when they discover the truth; this is what Sophocles did with Oedipus. Here indeed the relevant incident occurs outside the action of the play; but it may be a part of the tragedy, as with Alcmaeon in Astydamas's play, or Telegonus in *The Wounded Odysseus*. A third alternative is for someone who is about to do a terrible deed in ignorance of the relationship to discover the truth before he does it. These are the only possibilities, for the deed must either be done or not done, and by someone either with or without knowledge of the facts.

The least acceptable of these alternatives is when someone in possession of the facts is on the point of acting but fails to do so, for this merely shocks us, and, since no suffering is involved, it is not tragic. Hence nobody is allowed to behave like this, or only seldom, as when Haemon fails to kill Creon in the *Antigone*. Next in order of effectiveness is when the deed is actually done, and here it is better that the character should act in ignorance and only learn the truth afterwards, for there is nothing in this to outrage our feelings, and the revelation comes as a surprise. However, the best method is the last, when, for example, in the *Cresphontes* Merope intends to kill her son, but recognizes him and does not do so; or when the same thing happens with brother and sister in *Iphigenia in Tauris*; or when, in the *Helle*, the son recognizes his mother when he is just about to betray her.

This then is the reason why, as I said before, our tragedies keep to a few families. For in their search for dramatic material it was by chance rather than by technical knowledge that the poets discovered how to gain tragic effects in their plots. And they are still obliged to have recourse to those families in which sufferings of the kind I have described have been experienced.

I have said enough now about the arrangement of the incidents in a tragedy and the type of plot it ought to have.

CHAPTER 15

The Characters of Tragedy

In characterization there are four things to aim at. First and foremost, the characters should be good. Now character will be displayed, as I have pointed out, if some preference is revealed in speech or action, and if it is a preference for what is good the character will be good. There can be goodness in every class of person; for instance, a woman or a slave may be good, though the one is possibly an inferior being and the other in general an insignificant one.

In the second place the portrayal should be appropriate. For example, a character may possess manly qualities, but it is not appropriate that a female character should be given manliness or cleverness.

Thirdly, the characters should be lifelike. This is not the same thing as making them good, or appropriate in the sense in which I have used the word.

And fourthly, they should be consistent. Even if the person who is being represented is inconsistent, and this trait is the basis of his character, he must nevertheless be portrayed as consistently inconsistent.

As an example of unnecessary badness of character, there is Menelaus in the *Orestes*. The character who behaves in an unsuitable and inappropriate way is exemplified in Odysseus' lament in the *Scylla*, and in Melanippe's speech. An inconsistent character is shown in *Iphigenia at Aulis*, for Iphigenia as a suppliant is quite unlike what she is later.

As in the arrangement of the incidents, so too in characterization one must always bear in mind what will be either necessary or probable; in other words, it should be necessary or probable that such and such a person should say or do such and such a thing, and similarly that this particular incident should follow on that.

Furthermore, it is obvious that the unravelling of the plot should arise from the circumstances of the plot itself, and not be brought about *ex machina*, as is done in the *Medea* and in the episode of the embarkation in the *Iliad*. The *deus ex machina* should be used only for matters outside the play proper, either for things that happened before it and that cannot be known by the human characters, or for things that are yet to come and that require to be foretold prophetically – for we allow to the gods the power to see all things. However, there should be nothing inexplicable about what happens, or if there must be, it should be kept outside the tragedy, as is done in Sophocles's *Oedipus*.[1]

Since tragedy is a representation of people who are better than the average, we must copy the good portrait-painters. These, while reproducing the distinctive appearance of their sitters and making likenesses, paint them better-looking than they are. In the same way the poet, in portraying men who are hot-tempered, or phlegmatic, or who have other defects of character, must bring out these qualities in them, and at the same time show them as decent people, as Agathon and Homer have portrayed Achilles.

These points must be carefully watched, as too must those means used to appeal to the eye, which are necessarily dependent on the poet's art; for here too it is often possible to make mistakes. However, enough has been said about these matters in my published works.

1. Aristotle is here referring to the fact that Oedipus remained for many years ignorant of the circumstances of Laius's death. Cf. Chapter 24, p. 70.

CHAPTER 16

The Different Kinds of Discovery

I HAVE already explained what I mean by discovery. Of the different kinds of discovery, the first is the least artistic, and is mostly used from sheer lack of invention; this is discovery by means of visible signs or tokens. These may be congenital marks, like 'the spearhead that the Earthborn bear', or 'stars', such as those that Carcinus uses in his *Thyestes*; or they may be acquired, whether marks on the body such as scars, or external objects such as necklaces – or, in the *Tyro*, the discovery by means of the cradle. However, some ways of using these tokens are better than others; for example, the discovery of Odysseus through his scar is made in one way by his nurse and in another way by the swineherds. These discoveries, when made merely to gain credence, are less effective, as are all types of discovery used for such intentions; better are those that are unexpected, as happens in the Washing Episode in the *Odyssey*.

The second class of discoveries are those which are manufactured by the poet, and which are inartistic for that reason. An example occurs in *Iphigenia in Tauris* when Orestes reveals who he is. While the identity of Iphigenia is revealed by means of the letter, Orestes himself is made to say what the poet here requires instead of its being done through the plot; and this is not far removed from the fault I spoke about a moment ago, for he might have brought some tokens as well. Another example is 'the voice of the shuttle' in Sophocles's *Tereus*.

A third kind is the discovery that is due to memory, when the sight of something leads to the required understanding. Thus in *The Cyprians*, by Dicaeogenes, Teucer bursts into tears on seeing the portrait, and in *The Tale of Alcinous* Odysseus also weeps when the sound of the minstrel's harp reawakens the past for him, and this is how these two are recognized.

The fourth kind is the result of reasoning, such as is found in *The Choephori*: 'Someone who is like me has come; no one is like me except Orestes; therefore it is Orestes who has come.'

Another example is what the sophist Polyidus suggests for the *Iphigenia*, for it is likely enough that Orestes should reason that, as his sister was sacrificed, so too it was his fate to be sacrificed. Then there is the episode in the *Tydeus* of Theodectes when the father has come to find his son, and realizes that he is himself to die; or that in the *Phineidae* where, on seeing a particular place, the women infer that they are fated to die there, for it was there that they had been exposed at birth.

There is also a fictitious form of discovery arising from the fallacious reasoning of the parties concerned, as in *Odysseus the False Messenger*; he said that he would know the bow, which he had not seen; but it was false reasoning to suppose from this that he would know it again.[1]

Of all the forms of discovery, the best is that which is brought about by the incidents themselves, when the startling disclosure results from events that are probable, as happens in Sophocles's *Oedipus*, and again in the *Iphigenia* – for it was quite probable that she should wish to send off a letter. Discovery scenes of this kind are the only ones that dispense with such artificial aids as tokens and necklaces. The next best are those that depend on reasoning.

CHAPTER 17

Some Rules for the Tragic Poet

In putting together his plots and working out the kind of speech to go with them, the poet should as far as possible keep the scene before his eyes. In this way, seeing everything very vividly, as though he were himself an eyewitness of the events, he will find what is appropriate, and will be least likely to overlook inconsistencies. Evidence of this is the censure laid on Carcinus, by whom Amphiaraus was made to come out of a temple; this would have escaped notice if the episode had not

1. The text here seems to be defective, and it is difficult to render it satisfactorily. Bywater translates: 'He said he should know the bow – which he had not seen; but to suppose from that that he would know it again (as though he had once seen it) was bad reasoning.'

been actually seen, but the audience took offence at it, and the play was not a success on the stage.

As far as possible, too, the dramatic poet should carry out the appropriate gestures as he composes his speeches, for of writers with equal abilities those who can actually make themselves feel the relevant emotions will be the most convincing – agitation or rage will be most vividly reproduced by one who is himself agitated or in a passion. Hence poetry is the product either of a man of great natural ability or of one not wholly sane; the one is highly responsive, the other possessed.

As for the stories, whether he is taking over something ready-made or inventing for himself, the poet should first plan in general outline, and then expand by working out appropriate episodes. What I mean by planning in outline may be illustrated from the *Iphigenia*, as follows: A young girl was offered as a sacrifice, and mysteriously disappeared from the view of her sacrificers; she was set down in another country, where it was the custom to sacrifice strangers to the goddess, and became the priestess of this rite. Some time later it happened that the priestess's brother arrived (the fact that the oracle had for a certain reason told him to go there and the purpose of his journey are matters that lie outside the plot). On his arrival he was seized, and was about to be sacrificed, when he revealed who he was, either in the way that Euripides makes it happen or, as Polyidus suggests, by making the not unnatural remark that not only his sister, it seemed, was fated to be sacrificed, but himself too; and thus he was saved.

When he has reached this stage the poet may supply the proper names and fill in the episodes, making sure that they are appropriate, like the fit of madness in Orestes which led to his capture, and his escape by the device of the purification.

In plays the episodes are of course short; in epic poetry they are what supply the requisite length. The story of the *Odyssey*, for example, is not a long one. A man is kept away from his home for many years; Poseidon is watching him with a jealous eye, and he is alone. The state of affairs at home is that his wealth is being squandered by his wife's suitors, and plots are being laid against his son's life. After being buffeted by many storms he returns home and reveals his identity; he falls upon his enemies and destroys them, but preserves his own life. There you have the essential story of the *Odyssey*; the rest of the poem is made up of episodes.

CHAPTER 18

Further Rules for the Tragic Poet

EVERY tragedy has its complication and its denouement. The complication consists of the incidents lying outside the plot, and often some of those inside it, and the rest is the denouement. By complication I mean the part of the story from the beginning to the point immediately preceding the change to good or bad fortune; by denouement the part from the onset of this change to the end. In the *Lynceus* of Theodectes, for instance, the complication is what happened before the events of the play proper, together with the seizure of the boy and that in turn of the parents, and the denouement extends from the accusation of murder to the end.

Properly speaking, tragedies should be classed as similar or dissimilar according to their plots, that is to say, according to their similarity in complication and denouement. Many poets are skilful in complicating their plots but clumsy in unravelling them; a constant mastery of both techniques is what is required.

There are four kinds of tragedy, a number corresponding to that of the constituent parts that I spoke about. There is complex tragedy, which depends entirely on reversal and discovery; tragedy of suffering, as in the various plays on Ajax or Ixion; tragedy of character, as in *The Phthiotides* and the *Peleus*; and fourthly, spectacular tragedy, as in *The Phorcides*, in the *Prometheus*, and in plays with scenes in Hades. The poet should try to include all these elements, or, failing that, as many as possible of the most important, especially since it is the fashion nowadays to find fault with poets; just because there have been poets who excelled in the individual parts of tragedy, the critics expect that a single man should outdo each of them in his special kind of excellence.

Bearing in mind what has often been said, the dramatic poet

must be careful not to give his tragedy an epic structure, by which I mean one with a multiplicity of stories – as though one were to attempt a plot covering the whole story of the *Iliad*. By reason of its length, the *Iliad* can allow the proper development of its various parts, but in plays the results of such attempts are disappointing, as is proved by experience. For all the poets who have dramatized the destruction of Troy in its entirety, and not, like Euripides, only parts of it, or the whole of the story of Niobe, and not as Aeschylus did it, have either failed utterly or done badly in the dramatic competitions; and indeed even a play by Agathon was a failure for this alone. And yet in the handling of reversals and of simple plots these poets may succeed wonderfully in getting the effect they want, that is, one which is tragic and appeals to our humanity. This happens when the clever man who is also wicked is outwitted, as Sisyphus was, or when the brave man who is also unscrupulous is worsted; and this is a likely enough result, as Agathon points out, for it is quite likely that many things should happen contrary to likelihood.

The Chorus should be regarded as one of the actors; it should be a part of the whole, and should assume a share in the action, as happens in Sophocles, but not in Euripides. With other playwrights the choral songs may have no more to do with the plot in hand than with any other tragedy; they are mere choral interludes, according to the practice first introduced by Agathon. But what difference is there between the singing of interpolated songs like these and the transference of a speech or a whole episode from one play to another?

CHAPTER 19

Thought and Diction

Now that the other parts of tragedy have been dealt with, it remains to say something about diction and thought. As far as thought is concerned, enough has been said about it in my treatise on rhetoric, for it more properly belongs to that study. Thought includes all the effects that have to be produced by means of language; among these are proof and refutation, the awakening of emotions such as pity, fear, anger, and the like, and also exaggeration and depreciation. It is clear, too, that in the action of the play the same principles should be observed whenever it is necessary to produce effects of pity or terror, or of greatness or probability – with this difference, however, that here the effects must be made without verbal explanation, while the others are produced by means of language coming from the lips of a speaker, and are dependent on the use of language. For where would be the need of a speaker if the required effects could be conveyed without the use of language?

As for diction, one branch of study is the various forms of expression, an understanding of which belongs to the art of elocution and is necessary to the practitioner of this art: I refer to such things as a command, a prayer, a statement, a threat, a question, an answer, and so on. The poet's art is not seriously criticized according to his knowledge or ignorance of these things. For what would anyone think is wrong about the words which Protagoras censures on the grounds that the poet, intending a prayer, actually gives a command when he says, 'Sing of the wrath, Goddess'? For, says Protagoras, to order a person to do or not to do something is a command. However, we may pass this topic over as one which, though it may be relevant to some other art, is not so to the art of poetry.

CHAPTER 20

Some Linguistic Definitions

LANGUAGE in general is made up of the following parts: the letter, the syllable, the connecting-word, the article, the noun, the verb, the inflexion or case, and the phrase or proposition.

A letter is an indivisible sound, not just any such sound, but one from which intelligible language may be produced; animals also, it is true, utter indivisible sounds, but none that I should describe as a letter. The different forms of this sound are the vowel, the semi-vowel, and the mute letter or consonant. A vowel is a letter which has an audible sound without any contact between two of the organs of speech. A semi-vowel (S or R, for instance) is given audible sound by such a contact. A mute is a letter which even with such contact has no sound of its own, but which becomes audible when combined with letters which possess sound; examples are G and D. The letters differ in sound according to the shape of the mouth and the places where they are produced; according as they are aspirated or not aspirated; according to their length or shortness; according as they have an acute, a grave, or a circumflex accent. However, the detailed study of these matters is the province of the metrist.

A syllable is a sound-unit without meaning, made up of a mute and a sounded letter; for GR without an A is as much a syllable as it is with an A, as in GRA. But these distinctions are also the concern of metrical theory.

A connecting-word is a sound-unit without significance which neither hinders nor helps the production of a single significant utterance from the combination of several sounds, and which should not be put at the beginning of a phrase standing by itself; examples are *μέν*, *δή*, *τοί*, and *δέ*.[1] Alternatively it is a sound without significance capable of producing a single significant utterance from the combination of several sounds which are themselves significant; examples are *ἀμφί* and *περί* and similar words.[2]

An article is a sound without significance which indicates the beginning or the end of a speech, or a dividing-point in it, and its natural position is at either end or in the middle.

A noun is a composite of sounds with a meaning; it is independent of time, and none of its individual parts has a meaning in its own right. For in compounds we do not give separate meanings to the parts; in the name 'Theodore', for instance, the *dore* part has in itself no meaning.

A verb is a composite of sounds with a meaning; it is concerned with time, and, as was the case with nouns, none of its

1. These particles, though virtually untranslatable by single English words, indicate particular relationships between the phrases or clauses that they link.

2. Both words (*amphi*, *peri*) mean 'about', 'around', and they are presumably connecting-words in that they are prepositions linking words in special relationships.

individual parts has a meaning in its own right. The words 'man' and 'white' give no indication of time, but 'walks' and 'has walked' indicate respectively present and past time.

Case or inflexion in a noun or verb is that which gives the sense of 'of' or 'to' a thing, and the like, or indicates whether it relates to one or many, as with 'man' and 'men'. Alternatively it may signify types of intonation, as in question or command; 'walked?' and 'walk!' represent verbal inflexions of this kind.

A phrase or proposition is a composite of sounds with a meaning, and some parts of it have a meaning of their own. Not every proposition is made up of verbs and nouns – the definition of a man, for example; it is possible for a proposition to exist without verbs, and yet some part of it will always have a meaning of its own, as 'Cleon' has in the proposition 'Cleon walks'. A proposition may represent unity in one of two ways, either in that it implies one thing, or in that it achieves unity by a conjunction of several factors; the unity of the *Iliad*, for example, results from such a conjunction, that of the definition of a man from its signifying one thing.

CHAPTER 21

Poetic Diction

NOUNS may be classified as simple, by which I mean those made up of elements which individually have no meaning, like the word 'earth' (*γῆ*), or as double or compound. These compounds may take the form either of a part which has a meaning combined with one which has no meaning – although within the compound no part has a separate meaning – or of parts which all have meanings. A noun may be triple or quadruple or multiple in form, like many of our more grandiose names, for example, Hermocaïcoxanthus.

Every noun is either a word in current use or a foreign loan-word, a metaphor or an ornamental word, a poetic coinage or a word that has been expanded or abbreviated or otherwise altered.

By a word in current use I mean a word that everybody uses,

and by a loan-word one that other peoples use. Obviously the same word can be both current and a loan-word, though not in relation to the same people; to the Cypriots, for example, *sigunon* is the current word for a spear, but to us it is a loan-word.

Metaphor is the application to one thing of a name belonging to another thing; the transference may be from the genus to the species, from the species to the genus, or from one species to another, or it may be a matter of analogy. As an example of transference from genus to species I give 'Here lies my ship', for lying at anchor is a species of lying. Transference from species to genus is seen in 'Odysseus has indeed performed ten thousand noble deeds', for 'ten thousand', which is a particular large number, is used here instead of the word 'many'. Transference from one species to another is seen in 'Draining off the life with the bronze' and 'Severing with the unyielding bronze'; here 'draining off' is used for 'severing', and 'severing' for 'draining off', and both are species of 'taking away'.

I explain metaphor by analogy as what may happen when of four things the second stands in the same relationship to the first as the fourth to the third; for then one many speak of the fourth instead of the second, and the second instead of the fourth. And sometimes people will add to the metaphor a qualification appropriate to the term which has been replaced. Thus, for example, a cup stands in the same relationship to Dionysus as a shield to Ares, and one may therefore call the cup Dionysus's shield and the shield Ares's cup. Or again, old age is to life as evening is to day, and so one may call the evening the old age of the day, or name it as Empedocles named it[1]; and one may call old age the evening of life or the sunset of life. In some cases there is no name for some of the terms of the analogy, but the metaphor can be used just the same. For example, to scatter corn is called sowing, but there is no word for the sun's scattering of its flame; however, this stands in the same relationship to sunlight as sowing does to corn, and hence the expression, 'sowing his god-created flame'.

This kind of metaphor can also be used in another way;

1. The words that Empedocles used in this connexion are not extant; they must have been something like, but not identical with, 'the old age of the day'.

having called an object by the name of something else, one can deny it one of its attributes – for example, call the shield, not Ares's cup, but a wineless cup.

A poetic coinage is a word which has not been in use among a people, but has been invented by the poet himself. There seem to be words of this kind, such as 'sprouters' for horns, and 'supplicator' for priest.

A word is expanded when it uses a longer vowel than is normal to it or takes on an extra syllable, and it is abbreviated when some part of it has been removed. Examples of expansion are *πόληος* for *πολέως* and *Πηληιάδεω* for *Πηλείδου*, and of abbreviation *κρῖ* and *δῶ*, and *ὄψ* in *μία γίνεται ἀμφοτέρων ὄψ* ('the faces of the pair become as one').[1] An altered word is one in which part is left unchanged and part is coined, as when *δεξιτερόν* is used for *δεξιόν* in *δεξιτερὸν κατὰ μαζόν* ('on the right breast').

Of the nouns themselves some are masculine, some feminine, and some neuter. Masculine are all that end in N (n), P (r), and *Σ* (s), and in the compounds of *Σ*, that is, the two letters *Ψ* (ps) and *Ξ* (x). Feminine are all those ending in the vowels that are always long, such as H (*ē*) and *Ω* (*ō*), and in A among the vowels which may be lengthened. Thus there are equal numbers of masculine and feminine endings, for *Ψ* and *Ξ* are equivalent to *Σ*. No noun ends in a mute consonant or in a short vowel. Only three end in *i*: *μέλι* ('honey'), *κόμμι* ('gum'), and *πέπερι* ('pepper'); and five end in *Υ* (u). The neuters may end in these vowels, and in N (n), P (r), and *Σ* (s).

CHAPTER 22

Diction and Style

THE greatest virtue of diction is to be clear without being commonplace. The clearest diction is that which consists of words in everyday use, but this is commonplace, as can be seen

1. The expanded and normal genitive singular forms of *πόλις* ('city') and *Πηλείδης* ('son of Peleus') and the abbreviated *κρῖ* for *κριθή* ('barley'), *δῶ* for *δῶμα* ('house'), and *ὄψ* for *ὄψις* ('eye', 'face').

in the poetry of Cleophon and Sthenelus. On the other hand, a diction abounding in unfamiliar usages has dignity, and is raised above the everyday level. By unfamiliar usages I mean loan-words, metaphors, expanded forms, and anything else that is out of the ordinary. However, the exclusive use of forms of this kind would result either in a riddle or in barbarism – a riddle if they were all metaphorical, barbarism if they were all importations. The very essence of a riddle is to express facts in an impossible combination of language. This cannot be done by a mere succession of ordinary terms, but it can by the use of metaphors, as in the riddle, 'I saw a man welding bronze on another man with fire'[1] and similar examples. In the same way, the use of importations leads to barbarism. What is needed, then, is some mixture of these various elements. For the one kind will prevent the language from being mean and commonplace, that is, the unusual words, the metaphors, the ornamental terms, and the other figures I have described, while the everyday words give the necessary clarity.

Among the most effective means of achieving both clarity of diction and a certain dignity is the use of expanded, abbreviated, and altered forms of words; the unfamiliarity due to this deviation from normal usages will raise the diction above the commonplace, while the retention of some part of the normal forms will make for clarity. It is not good criticism, therefore, to censure this type of language and to ridicule the poet for using it, as the elder Eucleides did when he said that it would be easy to write poetry if one were allowed to lengthen syllables whenever one liked, and when he burlesqued this style in the lines, *'Επιχάρην εἶδον Μαραθῶναδε βαδίζοντα,* and *οὐκ ἄν γ' ἐράμενος τὸν ἐκείνου ἐλλέβορον.*[2]

1. The solution to this riddle is a bronze cupping-bowl. Heated and placed over a small incision, it would as it cooled draw out the blood.

2. The text is corrupt, and translators usually make no attempt to translate the two quotations, though the first may perhaps be rendered, 'I saw Epichares on his way to Marathon.' However, Aristotle's point is probably clear enough without translation. Homer occasionally lengthens a short vowel 'by position', as when he begins *Odyssey* XII, 423 with ἐπίτονος; no doubt other poets did so more frequently. Eucleides burlesques this practice by devising passages which can be read as verse if several short vowels are lengthened.

The too obvious use of these tricks, then, is ridiculous; moderation is necessary in all kinds of writing alike. The same effect would be produced by anyone using metaphors, unfamiliar loan-words and other such devices ineptly and for the mere sake of raising a laugh. How great a difference is made by their being used properly may be seen in epic poetry if one replaces them with ordinary everyday words in the verse; anyone substituting common words for the unfamiliar words or for the metaphors and other devices mentioned would see the truth of what I am saying. For instance, Aeschylus and Euripides wrote the same line of iambics, with the change only of a single word; an unfamiliar word was substituted for an ordinary one, and the new line is beautiful where the old was commonplace. This was the line as Aeschylus wrote it in his *Philoctetes*:

> φαγέδαινα ἥ μου σάρκας ἐσθίει ποδός.[1]

For ἐσθίει ('eats') Euripides put θοινᾶται ('feasts upon'). Just suppose that in the line

> νῦν δέ μ' ἐὼν ὀλίγος τε καὶ οὐτιδανὸς καὶ ἀεικής[2]

one were to use everyday words and say,

> νῦν δέ μ' ἐὼν μικρός τε καὶ ἀσθενικὸς καὶ ἀειδής.

Or suppose that for this line,

> δίφρον ἀεικέλιον καταθεὶς ὀλίγην τε τράπεζαν,[3]

one were to read

> δίφρον μοχθηρὸν καταθεὶς μικράν τε τράπεζαν.

Or that for ἠιόνες βοόωσιν ('the sea-shore is thundering') one were to read ἠιόνες κράζουσιν ('the sea-shore is crying out').

1. 'The ulcer that eats the flesh of my foot.' The Philoctetes plays of Aeschylus and Euripides are lost.

2. *Odyssey* IX, 515 (except that ἄκικυς has been misquoted as ἀεικής). 'And now a puny fellow, ungoodly and of no account, [has blinded me].' Aristotle's inferior version might be rendered, 'And now a little, weak, ugly fellow ...'.

3. *Odyssey* XX, 259. 'Having placed for him an unseemly stool and an insignificant table.' In the inferior version, 'Having placed for him a shabby stool and a little table.'

Then again, Ariphrades ridiculed the tragedians for using expressions that no one would use in ordinary speech, such as *δωμάτων ἄπο* ('from the houses away') instead of *ἀπὸ δωμάτων* ('away from the houses'), and *σέθεν* ('thine'), and *ἐγὼ δέ νιν* ('I [married] her'), and *Ἀχιλλέως πέρι* instead of *περὶ Ἀχιλλέως* ('about Achilles'), and the like. By the very fact of not being normal idiom, all such usages as these raise the diction above the level of the commonplace; but Ariphrades failed to see this.

It is a fine thing to be able to make proper use of all the devices I have mentioned, as also of compound words and unfamiliar importations, but far the most important thing to master is the use of metaphor. This is the one thing that cannot be learnt from anyone else, and it is the mark of great natural ability, for the ability to use metaphor well implies a perception of resemblances.

Of the different types of words, compound forms are best suited to dithyrambs, unfamiliar borrowings to heroic verse, and metaphorical usages to iambic verse. All these may, indeed, be fittingly used in heroic verse; but in iambic verse, which as far as possible models itself on speech, the only appropriate terms are those that anyone might use in speeches, and these are words in current use, metaphors, and ornamental words.

I need say no more now about tragedy and the art of representation by means of action.

CHAPTER 23

Epic Poetry

As for the art of representation in the form of narrative verse, clearly its plots should be dramatically constructed, like those of tragedies; they should centre upon a single action, whole and complete, and having a beginning, a middle, and an end, so that like a single complete organism the poem may produce its own special kind of pleasure. Nor should epics be constructed like the common run of histories, in which it is not the exposition of a single action that is required, but of a single period, and of everything that happened to one or more persons during this period, however unrelated the various events may have been. For just as the sea-battle at Salamis and the engagement with the Carthaginians in Sicily took place at the same time, but did not work towards the same end, so too in any sequence of time events may follow one another without producing any one single result. Yet most of our poets use the methods of the historian.

In this respect, too, Homer seems, as I have already described him, divinely inspired beyond all other poets, in that, although the Trojan War had a beginning and an end, he did not attempt to put the whole of it into his poem; it would have been too large a subject to be taken in all at once, and, if he had limited its length, the diversity of its incident would have made it too complicated. As it is, he has selected one part of the story, and has introduced many incidents from other parts as episodes, such as the Catalogue of Ships and other episodes with which he gives variety to the poem. Other epic poets write about one man, or a single period of time, or a single action made up of many separate incidents; among such poets are the authors of the *Cypria* and *The Little Iliad*. Thus, while only one tragedy could be made out of the *Iliad* or the *Odyssey*, several might be made out of the *Cypria*, and more than eight out of *The Little Iliad*: an *Award of the Arms*, a *Philoctetes*, a *Neoptolemus*, an *Eurypylus*, an *Odysseus the Beggar*, a *Laconian Women*, a *Sack of Troy*, and a *Departure of the Fleet*, not to mention a *Sinon* and a *Trojan Women*.

CHAPTER 24

Epic Poetry (Continued)

FURTHERMORE, epic poetry must divide into the same types as tragedy, that is, the simple, the complex, that which turns on character, and that which turns on suffering. With the exception of song and spectacle, its constituent parts must also be the same, for it needs reversals and discoveries and tragic incidents, and moreover the thought and diction must be of good quality. All these things Homer was the first to use, and he did so with skill. Of his two poems the one, the *Iliad*, is simple in structure and a story of suffering, the other, the *Odyssey*, is complex (for it has discovery scenes throughout) and turns on character; moreover, they surpass all other poems in diction and in quality of thought.

Epic differs from tragedy both in the length of the composition and in the metre used. The limitations as to length that have already been indicated will suffice; that is to say, it must be possible for the beginning and the end to be embraced within a single view, and this will be the case if the poems are shorter than the ancient epics, but stretch to the length of a group of tragedies offered at a single hearing. It is the special advantage of epic that it may be of considerable length. In tragedy it is not possible to represent several parts of the story as taking place simultaneously, but only the part that is actually being performed on the stage by the actors; epic poetry, on the other hand, being narrative, is able to represent many incidents that are being simultaneously enacted, and, provided they are relevant, they increase the weight of the poem, and give it the merits of grandeur, variety of interest, and diversity in its episodes. Monotony will soon bore an audience and ruin the effect of a tragedy on the stage.

Experience has shown that the heroic hexameter is the right metre for epic. If anyone were to write a narrative poem in some other metre, or in a variety of metres, the incongruity would be glaring, for of all metres, the heroic hexameter has the greatest weight and stability, which enables it most readily to admit unfamiliar borrowings and metaphorical usages; and in this respect, too, the narrative form of representation is better than any other. The iambic and the trochaic tetrameter are metres suitable to the expression of movement, the latter being a dancing measure, while the former lends itself to the dramatic representation of action. However, it would be even more out of place to mix several metres, as Chaeremon did. And so no one has ever written a poem on the grand scale in any other than the heroic measure; as I have said, nature herself teaches us to choose the right metre for our purposes.

Admirable as he is in so many other respects, Homer is especially so in this: he is the only poet who recognizes what part he himself ought to play in his poems. The poet should speak as little as possible in his own person, for it is not in that way that he represents actions. Other poets appear in their own character throughout their poems, and little of what they write is impersonal representation. But after a few prefatory words, Homer at once introduces a man, a woman, or some other person, no one of them lacking in character but each with distinctive characteristics.

The marvellous should of course be represented in tragedy, but epic poetry, where the persons acting the story are not before our eyes, may include more of the inexplicable, which is the chief element in the marvellous. If it were brought on to the stage there would be something ridiculous about the pursuit of Hector, with the Greeks merely standing there instead of pursuing him, and Achilles restraining them with a shake of the head; in the poem the absurdity is not apparent. The marvellous is a source of pleasure, as is shown by the fact that in passing on a piece of news everyone will add something of his own as an agreeable extra.

Above all, Homer has taught other poets how to tell untruths as they ought to be told, that is, by the use of fallacy. If one thing exists because another exists, or happens because this other happens, people think that, if the consequent exists or happens, the antecedent will also exist; but this is not the case. Thus if a proposition were untrue, but there was something else which must be true or must happen if the proposition were true, then it is this something else that we should lay down as a fact; for the mind, knowing it to be true, may fallaciously infer the truth of the original proposition. There is an example of this in the episode of the Washing in the *Odyssey*.[1]

Probable impossibilities are to be preferred to improbable possibilities. Stories should not be made up of irrational incidents; anything irrational should as far as possible be excluded,

1. *Odyssey* XIX, 164–260. Odysseus tells Penelope that he is one Aethon, a Cretan, who entertained Odysseus when he was blown off his course on the way to Troy. She believes him because he accurately describes Odysseus's dress and appearance and his squire Eurybates. The fallacy is that she infers the truth of the antecedent from the truth of the consequent.

or if not, at least kept out of the tale proper, like Oedipus's not knowing how Laius died; not admitted into the play, as in the *Electra* we have the messenger's report of the Pythian Games, or in the *Mysians* the business of the man's coming from Tegea to Mysia without speaking. To say that otherwise the plot would have been spoilt is ridiculous; plots like these should not be devised in the first instance, but if a poet does employ such a plot and it appears that it could have been worked out more reasonably, then his endeavour is entirely misplaced. Even in the *Odyssey* the irrational elements in the episode of Odysseus's being set ashore in Ithaca would obviously not have been acceptable if they had been treated by an inferior poet; as it is, Homer has managed to disguise their absurdity, charming it away by his other excellences.[1]

The diction should be elaborated only in 'neutral' sections, that is, in passages where neither character nor thought is in question, for diction that is too brilliant may obscure the presentation of character and thought.

CHAPTER 25

Critical Objections and their Answers

THE way to get a clear idea of the various critical problems – their number, their nature, and the solutions to be offered – is to look at them as follows. Like the painter or any other artist, the poet aims at the representation of life; necessarily, therefore, he must always represent things in one of three ways: either as they were or are, or as they are said to be or seem to be, or as they ought to be. His medium is language, with the possible admixture of unfamiliar terms and metaphors and the various other modifications of language that we allow to poets. We must remember, too, that there are not the same standards of correctness in poetry as in political theory or any

1. *Odyssey* XIII, 116 ff. The critics considered it irrational that Odysseus should not have awakened when the Phaeacians ran their ship aground in the harbour of Phorcys in Ithaca and lifted him out on to the sand.

other art. In poetry there are two kinds of fault, the one kind essential, the other incidental. If the poet has undertaken to represent some particular fact, and has gone astray through sheer lack of skill, that is an essential fault. But if his error lies in what he sets out to do, if for instance he represents a horse with both its offside legs thrown forward, then that is an error in some special branch of knowledge (it could perhaps be medicine or some other technical subject); or alternatively impossibilities of some other kind may have been depicted, but no essential fault is involved. These then are the points to be considered in resolving problems of criticism.

Taking first problems relating to the essentials of the poetic art: if the poet has depicted something impossible, he is at fault indeed, but he is justified in doing it as long as the art attains its true end, as I have described it, that is, as long as it makes this or some other part of the poem more striking. The pursuit of Hector is a case in point. If, however, this end could have been achieved just as well, or better, by conforming to the requirements of the art, then there is no justification for the fault, for if possible a poem should be entirely free of faults. Then again, which of the two kinds of fault is actually in question, one that concerns the essentials of the poetic art or one that is merely incidental? It is a less serious fault not to know that a female deer has no horns than to make an unrecognizable picture of one.

Suppose next that a description is criticized as not being true. The answer might be, 'No, but it ought to be like that' – just as Sophocles said that he drew men as they ought to be, whereas Euripides drew them as they are. However, if neither of these claims fits the case, then an appeal might be made to tradition, as for example with the tales about the gods. Now it is possible that these tales are neither true nor improve on the truth, but are what Xenophanes said of them;[1] nevertheless they are in accordance with tradition. In other cases the answer might be, not that it is better than the truth, but that it represents things as they used to be – for instance in the matter of the

1. Xenophanes (sixth century B.C.) attacked the polytheism and anthropomorphism of the traditional Greek religion.

spears: 'Their spears stood upright on their butt ends'; for that was then the custom, as it still is among the Illyrians.

In deciding whether something that has been said or done is morally good or bad, not only should we pay regard to the goodness or badness of the saying or deed itself, but we should also take into account the persons by whom and to whom it was said or done, the occasion, the means, and the reason – whether, for example, to bring about a greater good, or to avert a greater evil.

Some criticisms may be answered by examining the diction; an example is the rare word in *οὐρῆας μὲν πρῶτον*, where it is possible that by *οὐρῆας* Homer means 'sentinels', not 'mules'. Then there is Dolon, *ὅς ῥ' ἦ τοι εἶδος μὲν ἔην κακός* ('who indeed was evil of form'); here the reference is perhaps not to his deformed body but to his ugly face, for the Cretans use *εὐειδές* ('fair-formed') with the sense of *εὐπρόσωπον* ('fair-faced'). Then again, *ζωρότερον δὲ κέραιε* ('stronger mix the wine') may mean 'more quickly mix the wine', and not have the sense of 'unmixed', as though for drunkards.

Other expressions are metaphorical. For example, in Homer's words, *ἄλλοι μέν ῥα θεοί τε καὶ ἀνέρες εὗδον* <*ἅπαντες*> *παννύχιοι*,[1] bearing in mind that he also says, *ἦ τοι ὅτ' ἐς πεδίον τὸ Τρωικὸν ἀθρήσειεν, αὐλῶν συρίγγων τε ὅμαδόν*, the word *ἅπαντες* ('all') is metaphorically used instead of *πολλοί* ('many'), for *πᾶν* ('all') is a species of *πολύ* ('much'). So too *οἴη δ' ἄμμορος* ('alone without a share)'[2] is metaphorical, for the best-known representative is referred to as the only one.

Again, the solution of the difficulty may be a matter of how to read a word, as with the changes of Hippias of Thasos in

1. *Iliad* II, 1–2. 'Then all other gods and men slept through the night.' The quotation differs slightly from our text of the *Iliad*; moreover, Aristotle seems to be confusing it with the very similar opening to *Iliad* X, since the quotation that follows ('And indeed when he gazed at the Trojan plain [Agamemnon wondered at] the sound of flutes and pipes and the noise [of men]') comes from lines 11–13 of that book. Aristotle's point is that 'all' is used metaphorically for 'many', for if the Trojans are revelling all men cannot be asleep.

2. *Iliad* XVIII, 489. 'She that alone has no share in the baths of the Ocean.' The reference is to the Great Bear; but as the other northern constellations also do not set, the reference to the Great Bear as the only one is metaphorical.

δίδομεν δέ οἱ ('and we grant him')[1] and τὸ μὲν οὗ καταπύθεται ὄμβρῳ ('part of which rots in the rain');[2] or again of word-grouping, as in Empedocles: αἶψα δὲ θνήτ' ἐφύοντο, τὰ πρὶν μάθον ἀθάνατα ζωρά τε πρὶν κέκρητο;[3] or of ambiguity, as in παρῴχηκεν δὲ πλέω νύξ,[4] where πλέω is ambiguous; or, finally, of normal linguistic usage – wine mixed with water, for example, is normally called wine, and so one finds the phrase 'a greave of newly-wrought tin'[5] and workers of metal are called blacksmiths, and so too Ganymede is said to pour wine for Zeus, although the gods do not drink wine.[6] But this may perhaps be explained as a metaphorical usage.

Whenever a word seems to involve some inconsistency of meaning, we ought to consider in how many ways it may be interpreted in the context – in, for example, τῇ ῥ' ἔσχετο χάλκεον ἔγχος ('there the brazen spear was stopped'), how many ways there are of taking 'there ... was stopped'.[7] We

1. The reference is to *Iliad* II, 15 – where, however, our text is different. Zeus is telling the Dream-god how to lure Agamemnon to disaster. By reading δίδομεν as διδόμεν Hippias turns it into an infinitive used as an imperative, which transfers the telling of a falsehood from Zeus to the Dream-god and thus preserves Zeus's reputation for veracity.

2. *Iliad* XXIII, 328. The reference is to an old withered stump which, Homer says, does not rot in the rain. This seems incredible. However, if Homer's οὐ ('not') is changed to οὗ ('of which'), as Aristotle quotes it, the difficulty is removed.

3. 'And soon they grew mortal that formerly learned immortal ways, and pure formerly intermingled.' This necessarily awkward translation illustrates what appears to be the problem of word-order at issue – whether 'formerly' is to be taken with 'pure' (as seems preferable), or with 'intermingled'. Empedocles is speaking of the elements.

4. *Iliad* X, 253. 'And the night has advanced more [than two thirds, but the third part is still left].' The difficulty is that, if *more* than two thirds had passed, a third could not be left. It has been suggested that πλέω is to be taken, not as 'more', but as 'full': 'the night has advanced full two thirds.'

5. The greaves are made of bronze, an alloy of tin and copper, which is here called by the name of the more important metal.

6. The gods drink nectar, not wine; but in accordance with what is said in Chapter 21, the drink is metaphorically called 'wine'.

7. *Iliad* XX, 272 – at the end of a passage describing how Achilles took on his shield a spear hurled with great force by Aeneas. The shield consisted of a layer of gold, two of bronze, and two of tin. Homer says

should think how best we shall avoid the fault described by Glaucon when he says that critics make unreasonable presuppositions, and go on to draw conclusions from their own adverse comments on the poet; if his words conflict with the conclusions they have thus reached, they censure him as though he had actually said what they ascribe to him. This is what has happened in the case of Icarius. Some critics believe that he was a Spartan, and therefore think it strange that Telemachus should not have met him when he went to Sparta. But the truth of the matter may be, as the Cephallenians say, that Odysseus married in their country, and that the name was Icadius, not Icarius. Thus it is probably through a mistake that this particular difficulty has arisen.

Generally speaking, then, the 'impossible' has to be justified on grounds either of poetic effect, or of an attempt to improve on reality, or of accepted tradition. As far as poetic effect is concerned, a convincing impossibility is preferable to an unconvincing possibility. Even though it is impossible that there should be such people as Zeuxis used to paint, yet it would be better if there were, for the ideal type ought to be surpassingly good.

Accepted tradition may justify the use of the irrational, as may the plea that there are times when it is not irrational, for it is probable enough that things should happen contrary to probability. Verbal inconsistencies should be examined in the same way as refutations in dialectical exercises in order to see whether the poet means the same thing, in the same relation and with the same significance as you mean yourself, before you blame him for contradicting either what he has himself said or what an intelligent man would assume to be true. However, irrationality and depravity are rightly censured when there is no need for them and they are not properly used, as no good use is made of the irrationality in Euripides's introduction of Aegeus in the *Medea*, or of the depravity of Menelaus in the *Orestes*.

There are, then, five grounds on which a passage may be

---

that the spear drove through two layers, but was held by the gold – which would presumably be the outside layer. Bywater's solution of the difficulty is the suggestion that the spear was in fact held by the gold, even though its point pierced to the layers beneath.

censured: that it is impossible, irrational, immoral, inconsistent, or technically at fault. And the answers are to be studied in the light of the twelve criteria that I have already enumerated.

CHAPTER 26

Epic and Tragedy Compared

IT may be asked which of the two forms of representation is the better, the epic or the tragic. If the better form is the less vulgar, and the less vulgar is always that which is designed to appeal to the better type of audience, then it is obvious that the form that appeals to everybody is extremely vulgar. And indeed, as though you will not see them unless they thrust themselves on your notice, performers are apt to go in for a great deal of unnecessary movement; bad flute-players, for instance, throw themselves about if they have to represent throwing a discus, and keep pulling at the leader of the Chorus if they are performing 'Scylla'. This is what tragedy is like, we are told; it corresponds with what the older actors thought of their successors – for Mynniscus used to call Callipides 'the Ape' on the grounds that he overacted grossly, and the same was said of Pindarus. The tragic art as a whole, then, stands in the same relationship to the epic as these more recent actors do to the earlier. Thus epic is said to appeal to cultivated readers who do not need the help of visible forms, while tragedy appeals to meaner minds. If then it is a vulgar art, it is obviously inferior to epic.

Now in the first place, this way of arguing is a criticism of acting, not of poetry, for it is also possible for a bard to exaggerate his gestures while reciting, as Sosistratus used to do, and for a singer too, like Mnasitheus the Opuntian. No more than every kind of dancing is every kind of movement to be rejected, but only that of the meaner types of people; Callipides was subjected to the same criticism that is levelled against some modern actors, that is, that they cannot act the parts of respectable women. For another thing, tragedy fulfils its own special function even without the help of action, and in just the same way as epic, for its quality can be seen from reading it. So that if tragedy is in other respects the higher of the two arts, this disadvantage is not necessarily inherent in it.[1]

In the second place, tragedy has everything that epic has, and it can even use the epic measure; and as a not inconsiderable addition, it offers scenic effects and music, the source of a distinct feeling of pleasure. Then the effect is as vivid when a play is read as when it is acted. Moreover, this form of imitation achieves its ends in shorter compass, and what is more compact gives more pleasure than what is extended over a long period. Just imagine the *Oedipus* of Sophocles spread out over as many lines as there are in the *Iliad*. Then there is less unity in the imitation of the epic poets, as is shown by the fact that any one work of this kind contains matter for several tragedies, so that, if these poets deal with a single plot, either it will appear truncated if it is briefly set out, or it will give the impression of being watered down if it observes the usual length of such poems; I mean one composed of several actions, such as the *Iliad* or the *Odyssey*, which have many parts, and each of a certain amplitude – and yet these poems are constructed as well as they could be, and each is, as far as this is possible, the representation of a single action.

If, therefore, tragedy is superior to epic in all these respects, and also in fulfilling its artistic function – for these forms of art ought to give, not just any kind of pleasure, but the kinds I have described – then obviously, in achieving its ends better than epic, it must be the better form of art.

This is all I have to say about tragedy and epic poetry, whether in general terms or in relation to their various forms and constituent parts; about the number and the characteristics of these parts; about the causes of their success or failure; and about the various critical problems and their solutions.

1. The disadvantage claimed for it, that it appeals to meaner minds.

HORACE

On the Art of Poetry

HORACE
On the Art of Poetry

SUPPOSING a painter chose to put a human head on a horse's neck, or to spread feathers of various colours over the limbs of several different creatures, or to make what in the upper part is a beautiful woman tail off into a hideous fish, could you help laughing when he showed you his efforts? You may take it from me, my friends, that a book will have very much the same effect as these pictures if, like a sick man's dreams, the author's idle fancies assume such a shape that it is impossible to make head or tail of what he is driving at. 'But,' you will say, 'the right to take liberties of almost any kind has always been enjoyed by painters and poets alike.' I know that; we poets do claim this licence, and in our turn we concede it to others, but not to the point of associating what is wild with what is tame, of pairing snakes with birds or lambs with tigers.

Works that begin impressively and with the promise of carrying on in the heroic strain often have one or two purple passages tacked on to catch the eye, giving a description of Diana's grove and altar, the meanderings of a stream through a picturesque countryside, the River Rhine, or a rainbow. But this is not the right place for things of that kind. Perhaps, too, you know how to paint a cypress; but what is the point of that if you are being paid to paint a shipwrecked man swimming for dear life? A potter sets out to make a two-handled wine-flagon: why, as his wheel spins, does it turn into an ordinary water-jug? In short, whatever you set your hand to, you must be single-minded about it and keep to the point.

Most of us poets, my friends, are led astray by our notions of the right way to go to work. I try my hardest to be succinct, and merely succeed in being obscure; I aim at smoothness, only to find that I am losing fire and energy. One poet sets out to achieve the sublime, and falls into turgidity; another is over-cautious, and, nervous of spreading his wings, never leaves the ground. Yet another, wishing to vary the monotony of his subject with something out of the ordinary, introduces a dolphin into his woods, or puts a boar among his waves. If art is lacking, the avoidance of a petty fault may lead to a serious imperfection.

At the end of the row of stalls down by the Aemilian gladiatorial school there is a craftsman in bronze who will mould fingernails and reproduce wavy hair to the life, but the total effect of his work is unsatisfactory because he cannot put together a complete figure. Now if I set out to write a poem, I would no more want to be like him than to have a crooked nose, much though I might be admired for my dark eyes and black hair.

Choose a subject that is suited to your abilities, you who aspire to be writers; give long thought to what you are capable of undertaking, and what is beyond you. A man who chooses a subject within his powers will never be at a loss for words, and his thoughts will be clear and orderly. The virtue and attraction of order, I think I am right in saying, is that the poet will at any moment be saying exactly what his poem at that moment requires; he will be keeping back points for the time being or leaving them out altogether, and showing what he thinks admirable and what beneath notice.

Furthermore, you will make an excellent impression if you use care and subtlety in placing your words and, by the skilful choice of setting, give fresh meaning to a familiar word. If it happens that you have to invent new terms for the discussion of abstruse topics, you will have a chance to coin words that were unknown to earlier generations of Romans,[1] and no one will object to your doing this, as long as you do it with discretion. New and recently-coined words will win acceptance if they are borrowed from Greek sources and drawn upon sparingly. And indeed, why should we Romans allow this privilege to Caecilius and Plautus, and refuse it to Virgil and Varius? Why should I be grudged the right to add a few words

1. Horace's words are *cinctutis . . . Cethegis*, 'the girdled Cethegi'. He is referring to the time, some 200 years earlier, when such men as M. Cornelius Cethegus (censor B.C. 209, consul 204) wore a kind of girdle or loin-cloth (*cinctus*) under the toga instead of the tunic of later, more effeminate times.

to the stock if I can, when the language of Cato and Ennius has enriched our native speech by the introduction of new terms? It has always been accepted, and always will be, that words stamped with the mint-mark of the day should be brought into currency. As the woods change their foliage with the decline of each year, and the earliest leaves fall,[1] so words die out with old age; and the newly born ones thrive and prosper just like human beings in the vigour of youth. We are all destined to die, we and all our works. Perhaps the land has been dug out and an arm of the sea let in, to give protection to our fleets from the northern gales (and what a royal undertaking this was!);[2] or a marsh, long a barren waste on which oars were plied, has been put under the plough and produces food for the neighbouring towns;[3] or a river has been made to change a course ruinous to the cornfields and turned into a straighter channel:[4] whatever they are, the works of men will pass away. How much less likely are the glory and grace of language to have an enduring life! Many terms that have now dropped out of use will be revived, if usage so requires, and others which are now in repute will die out; for it is usage which regulates the laws and conventions of speech.

Homer showed us in what metre the exploits of kings and commanders and the miseries of war were to be recorded. The elegiac couplet was first used as the vehicle for lament, but was later adopted for verses of thanksgiving; however, scholars argue about who devised this slighter elegiac form, and the case so far rests undecided. Archilochus invented the iambic measure as the weapon for furious satire; it was adopted both for comedy and for high tragedy, since it is appropriate for

1. In warm countries deciduous trees do not necessarily shed all their foliage in autumn, but the oldest leaves are likely to fall.

2. This may be a reference to the Portus Julius, an artificial harbour which Agrippa, the friend of Augustus and his admiral in the Battle of Actium, formed on the coast of Campania by constructing strong channels between Lake Lucrinus and the sea and between Lake Lucrinus and Lake Avernus.

3. Probably a reference to the draining of the Pontine Marshes, projected by Julius Caesar and perhaps partly carried out by Augustus.

4. Probably a reference to the straightening of the course of the Tiber – another of Julius Caesar's schemes carried out in the time of Augustus.

dialogue, is capable of drowning the noises of the audience,[1] and is by its nature well suited to accompany action. To lyrical poetry the Muse assigned the task of celebrating the gods and their offspring, the winner in a boxing-match, and the horse that led the field; the task, too, of singing the woes of young lovers and the pleasures of wine.[2] If I have not the ability and skill to adhere to these well-defined functions and styles of poetic forms, why should I be hailed as a poet? Why out of false shame should I prefer to remain ignorant rather than to learn my craft? A comic subject is not susceptible of treatment in a tragic style, and similarly the banquet of Thyestes cannot be fitly described in the strains of everyday life or in those that approach the tone of comedy. Let each of these styles be kept for the role properly allotted to it. Yet even comedy at times uses elevated language, and an angry Chremes rails in bombastic terms;[3] while in tragedy Telephus and Peleus often express their grief in prosaic language, and each of them in his poverty-stricken exile renounces his usual rant and his sesquipedalian words[4] when he wants to move the spectator's pity with his lamentation.

It is not enough that poems should have beauty; if they are to carry the audience with them, they must have charm as well. Just as smiling faces are turned on those who smile, so is sympathy shown with those who weep. If you want to move me to tears, you must first feel grief yourself; then, Telephus and Peleus, your misfortunes will grieve me too, whereas, if your speeches are out of harmony with your feelings, I shall either fall asleep or burst out laughing. Pathetic language is appropriate to the face of sorrow, and violent language to the

1. The murmur of an audience might drown any but the clearest elocution; the regularly recurring stress of the iambic line would contribute towards the required clarity.

2. Greek lyrical poetry included hymns to the gods and heroes, odes (such as those of Pindar) celebrating victories in the games, and amatory and convivial poems (such as those of Sappho, Alcaeus, and Anacreon).

3. Terence uses the name Chremes four times in his comedies, three times for old men. The reference is probably to the *Heautontimorumenos* V, iv, where the old man Chremes rails at his son.

4. *Sesquipedalia verba*: literally 'words a foot and a half long'. Telephus and Peleus provided subjects for several tragedies.

face of anger; a sportive diction goes with merry looks, and a serious with grave looks. For nature has so formed us that we first feel inwardly any change in our fortunes; it is she that cheers us or rouses us to anger, she that torments us and bows us to the ground with a heavy burden of sorrow, and it is only afterwards that she expresses these feelings in us by means of the tongue. If the speaker's words are out of key with his fortunes, a Roman audience will cackle and jeer to a man. It will make a great difference whether a god or a hero is speaking, a man of ripe years or a hot-headed youngster in the pride of youth, a woman of standing or an officious nurse, a roving merchant or a prosperous farmer, a Colchian or an Assyrian, a man from Thebes or one from Argos.

Either follow the beaten track, or invent something that is consistent within itself. If in your play you happen to be representing the illustrious Achilles, let him be energetic, passionate, ruthless, and implacable; let him say that laws are not meant for him, and think that everything must yield to the force of arms. See to it that Medea is fierce and indomitable, Ino tearful, Ixion faithless, Io a wanderer, and Orestes sorrowful. If you introduce an untried subject to the stage, or are so bold as to invent a new character, be sure that it remains the same all the way through as it was at the beginning, and is entirely consistent.

It is hard to be original in treating well-worn subjects,[1] and it is better for you to be putting a Trojan tale into dramatic form than that you should be first in the field with a theme hitherto unknown and unsung.[2] A theme that is familiar can be made your own property as long as you do not waste your time on a hackneyed treatment; nor should you try to render your original word for word like a slavish translator, or in imitating another writer plunge yourself into difficulties from which shame, or the rules you have laid down for yourself, prevent you from extricating yourself. And you must not, like

1. *Difficile est proprie communia dicere.* Some editors would translate *communia* as 'subjects of general interest', others as 'subjects not treated before'.

2. This passage suggests that the young Piso is actually writing, or intending to write, a play on a Homeric theme.

the cyclic poet of old,[1] begin: 'Of Priam's fate I'll sing and war's renown.' What will emerge that can live up to such extravagant promises? The mountains will fall into labour, and there will be born – an absurd little mouse. How much more to the purpose are the words of the man who makes no foolish undertakings: 'Sing for me, Muse, the man who, after the fall of Troy, made himself acquainted with the ways of many men and their cities.' This poet does not mean to let his flash of fire die away in smoke, but to make the smoke give way to light, when he may with striking effect relate his tales of wonder, tales of Antiphates and Scylla and Charybdis and the Cyclops. He does not trace Diomede's return right back to the death of Meleager, or the Trojan War to the twin eggs of Leda.[2] All the time he is hurrying on to the crisis, and he plunges his hearer into the middle of the story as if it were already familiar to him; and what he cannot hope to embellish by his treatment he leaves out. Moreover, so inventive is he, and so skilfully does he blend fact and fiction, that the middle is not inconsistent with the beginning, nor the end with the middle.

I will tell you what I, and with me the public as a whole, look for in a play. If you want an appreciative hearer who will wait for the curtain and remain in his seat until the player calls out, 'Give us your applause', you must note the behaviour of people of different ages, and give the right kind of manners to characters of varying dispositions and years. The child who has just learnt to speak and to plant his feet firmly on the ground loves playing with his friends, will fly into a temper and with as little reason recover from it, and will change every hour. The beardless youth who has at last got rid of his tutor finds his pleasures in horses and dogs and the grassy sports-fields of the Campus Martius; pliant as wax, he is easily persuaded to vicious courses, is irritable with his counsellors, slow to pro-

1. The cyclic poets were epic poets, probably later than Homer, who wrote upon legends connected with the Trojan and Theban wars. Their poems were arranged into cycles by the Alexandrian scholars.

2. That is, to the birth of Helen. Leda was visited by Zeus in the form of a swan, and brought forth two eggs, from one of which Helen issued, and from the other Castor and Pollux.

vide for his needs, lavish with his money, of high aspirations and passionate desires, and quick to abandon the objects of his fancy. When he is become a man in years and spirit, his inclinations change; he sets out to acquire wealth and influential connexions, aims at securing public offices, and is careful to avoid doing anything which he might later wish had been done otherwise. The old man is beset by many troubles; either he tries to make money, but holds back miserably when it comes his way and is afraid to use it, or he is cautious and faint-hearted in all his dealings; he puts things off, clings to his hopes, and remains inactive in an eager desire to prolong his life; he is obstinate, too, and querulous, and given to praising the days when he was a boy and criticizing and rebuking his juniors. Advancing years bring with them many blessings, but many of these are taken away in the decline of life. Thus, in order not to give a young man the characteristics of old age, or the child those of a grown man, we shall always dwell upon the qualities that are appropriate to a particular time of life.

An episode is either acted on the stage, or reported as having taken place. However, the mind is less actively stimulated by what it takes in through the ear than by what is presented to it through the trustworthy agency of the eyes – something that the spectator can see for himself. But you will not bring on to the stage anything that ought properly to be taking place behind the scenes, and you will keep out of sight many episodes that are to be described later by the eloquent tongue of a narrator. Medea must not butcher her children in the presence of the audience, nor the monstrous Atreus cook his dish of human flesh within public view, nor Procne be metamorphosed into a bird, nor Cadmus into a snake. I shall turn in disgust from anything of this kind that you show me.

If you want your play to be called for and given a second performance, it should not be either shorter or longer than five acts. A *deus ex machina* should not be introduced unless some entanglement develops which requires such a person to unravel it. And there should not be more than three speaking characters on the stage at the same time.[1]

The Chorus should sustain the role and function of an

1. Literally, 'And let not a fourth character strive to speak.'

actor, and should not sing anything between the acts that does not contribute to the plot and fit appropriately into it. It should side with the good characters and give them friendly advice, and should control those who are out of temper and show approval to those who are anxious not to transgress. It should commend moderation in the pleasures of the table, the blessings of law and justice, and times of peace when the gates lie open; it should respect confidences, and should pray and beseech the gods to let prosperity return to the wretched and desert the proud.

At one time the flute – not as now bound with brass and a rival to the trumpet, but simple and delicate in tone and with only a few stops – was of service in giving the note to the Chorus and accompanying it; and its soft music filled rows of seats that were not yet overcrowded, where an audience small enough to be counted came together – simple, thrifty folk, modest and virtuous in their ways. But when a conquering race began to extend its territories, and cities grew in size, and the tutelary deity could be propitiated without fear of censure by drinking in the daytime on festal occasions, a greater freedom was allowed in the choice both of rhythms and melodies. For what taste could be expected in a crowd of uneducated men enjoying a holiday from work, when country bumpkins rubbed shoulders with townsfolk, and slum-dwellers with men of rank? Thus the flute-player introduced wanton movements that were unknown in the style of earlier days, and trailed his robe as he made his way over the stage. The grave lyre, too, acquired new notes,[1] and a more abrupt type of eloquence brought with it a new style of speech in which wise saws and prophecies of the future caught the very manner of the Delphic oracle.[2]

The poet originally competed in tragic verse for the paltry prize of a goat;[3] soon he introduced wild and naked satyrs on to the stage, and without loss of dignity tried his hand at a

1. By the addition of further strings.

2. They became as obscure and unhelpful as the utterances of the Delphic oracle.

3. The derivation of the word 'tragedy' from τράγος (*tragos*, 'he-goat'), because the prize in the competition for tragedy was a he-goat, is no longer accepted. However, in the earliest stages of Greek tragedy the Chorus consisted of satyrs, the primitive, goat-like followers of Dionysus,

form of crude jesting; for an audience that was tipsy after observing the Bacchic rites and in a lawless mood could only be held by the attraction of some enticing novelty. But if jesters and mocking satyrs are to win approval, and a transition made from the serious to the light-hearted, it must be done in such a way that no one who has been presented as a god or hero, and who a moment ago was resplendent in purple and gold, is transported into a dingy hovel and allowed to drop into the speech of the back streets, or alternatively to spout cloudy inanities in an attempt to rise above vulgarity. Tragedy scorns to babble trivialities, and, like a married woman obliged to dance at a festival, will look rather shamefaced among the wanton satyrs. If ever I write satyric dramas, my dear fellows, I shall not be content to use merely the plain, unadorned language of everyday speech; I shall try not to depart so far from the tone of tragedy as to make no distinction between the speech of a Davus, or of a bold-faced Pythias who has managed to trick Simo out of a talent, and that of Silenus, who after all was the guardian and attendant of the young god Bacchus. I shall aim at a style that employs no unfamiliar diction, one that any writer might hope to achieve, but would sweat tears of blood in his efforts and still not manage it – such is the power of words that are used in the right places and in the right relationships, and such the grace that they can add to the commonplace when so used. If you are going to bring woodland fauns on to the stage, I do not think you should ever allow them to speak as though they had been brought up in the heart of the city; do not let them be too youthfully indiscreet in the lines you give them, or crack any filthy or obscene jokes. For such things give offence to those of knightly or freeborn rank and the more

no doubt clad in goat-skins. The satyr-play, which Horace goes on to discuss, was a short play appended to a tragic trilogy, usually dealing in comic fashion with a theme related to that of the trilogy, and having a Chorus of satyrs. The only complete surviving satyr-play is the *Cyclops* of Euripides, best known in Shelley's version and recently translated for the Penguin Classics by Roger Lancelyn Green. It is doubtful whether, as Horace suggests, the satyric drama came into being later than tragedy; the two forms seem rather to be different developments of the same origins. Little is known of satyric drama in Rome; perhaps Piso, or even Horace himself, was hoping to revive it.

substantial citizens; these men do not take kindly to what meets with the approval of the masses, the buyers of roast beans and chestnuts, nor do they give it a prize.

A long syllable following a short one is called an iambus, which is a fast-moving foot. From this the name 'trimeters' became attached to the iambic line, since it produced six beats; and the metre was the same throughout the line.[1] But not so very long ago, so that it might fall upon the ear with rather more weight and deliberation, the iambic line obligingly opened its ranks to the steady spondee, but did not extend its welcome to the point of giving way to it in the second or fourth foot. The true iambic measure is rarely found in the 'noble' trimeters of Accius; and on the verse, too, with which Ennius so ponderously burdened the stage lies the reproach of over-hasty and careless composition, or of ignorance of his art. Not everyone is critical enough to be aware of rhythmical faults in verse, and an indulgence has been shown to our Roman poets that true poets should not need. Is that a reason for loose and lawless writing on my part? Or should I assume that everyone will notice my transgressions, and therefore proceed cautiously, keeping within the bounds in which I may safely hope for indulgence? If I do so, I shall have escaped censure, indeed, but shall not have deserved any praise. For yourselves, my friends, you must give your days and nights to the study of Greek models. But, you will say, your grandfathers were enthusiastic about the versification and wit of Plautus. They were altogether too tolerant, not to say foolish, in their admiration of both these things in him, if you and I have any idea of how to discriminate between coarseness and graceful wit, and how to pick out the right rhythm both by counting and by ear.

Thespis is given the credit for having invented tragedy as a new genre;[2] he is said to have taken his plays about to be sung

1. *Cum . . . redderet* is usually translated '*although* it produced'. But Horace has called the iambus a fast-moving or light foot, and he seems to be saying that because of this lightness the six iambics give the effect of a trimeter, two iambics forming a *metrum*.

2. He did this by introducing an actor who was independent of the Chorus, and who could speak a prologue and engage in dialogue with the leader of the Chorus. Thus he made tragedy dramatic.

and acted on wagons by players whose faces were smeared with the lees of wine. After him came Aeschylus, who devised the mask and the dignified robe of tragedy; it was he who laid down a stage with planks of moderate size, and who introduced the grand style into tragedy and increased the actor's height with buskins. These playwrights were succeeded by those of the Old Comedy, which enjoyed a fairly considerable favour; but its freedom degenerated into an offensive violence of language which had to be curbed by law. This law was observed, and the Chorus, deprived of its right to be abusive, fell into a shamed silence.

Our own poets have tried their hand in every style; and they have enjoyed some of their greatest successes when they have had the courage to turn aside from the paths laid down by the Greeks and sing of deeds at home, and this in both tragedies and comedies with Roman backgrounds. Indeed Italy would be no less renowned in the arts of language than she is in valour and the arts of war, were it not that her poets, one and all, shrink from the tedious task of polishing their work. But you, my dear fellows, the descendants of Numa Pompilius, you must have nothing to do with any poem that has not been trimmed into shape by many a day's toil and much rubbing out, and corrected down to the smallest detail.

Because Democritus believes that native genius is worth any amount of piddling art, and will not allow a place on Mount Helicon to poets with rational minds, a good many will not take the trouble to trim their nails and their beards; they haunt solitary places, and keep away from the public baths. For they will gain the repute and title of poets, they think, if they never submit to the ministrations of the barber Licinus a head that all the hellebore of all the Anticyras in the world could never reduce to sanity.[1] What an ass I am to purge the bile out of my system as the season of spring comes along! Otherwise no man would write better poetry. But the game's not worth the candle. So I will play the part of a whetstone, which can put an edge on a blade, though it is not itself capable of cutting. Even if I write nothing myself, I will teach the poet his duties and

1. Hellebore, which grew abundantly at Anticyra in Phocis, was prescribed as a cure for madness.

obligations; I will tell him where to find his resources, what will nourish and mould his poetic gift, what he may, and may not, do with propriety, where the right course will take him, and where the wrong.

The foundation and fountain-head of good composition is a sound understanding. The Socratic writings will provide you with material, and if you look after the subject-matter the words will come readily enough. The man who has learnt his duty towards his country and his friends, the kind of love he should feel for a parent, a brother, and a guest, the obligations of a senator and of a judge, and the qualities required in a general sent out to lead his armies in the field – such a man will certainly know the qualities that are appropriate to any of his characters. I would lay down that the experienced poet, as an imitative artist, should look to human life and character for his models, and from them derive a language that is true to life. Sometimes a play that has a few brilliant passages showing a true appreciation of character, even if it lacks grace and has little depth or artistry, will catch the fancy of an audience, and keep its attention more firmly than verse which lacks substance but is filled with well-sounding trifles.

To the Greeks the Muses gave native wit and the ability to turn phrases, and there was nothing they craved more than renown. We Romans in our schooldays learn long calculations for dividing the pound into dozens of parts. 'Here, young Albinus, you tell me: if you take an ounce from five-twelfths of a pound, what's left? Come on now, you could have answered by now.' 'A third of a pound.' 'Good! You'll be able to look after yourself all right. If you add an ounce, what does that come to?' 'A half.' When once this corroding lust for profit has infected our minds, can we hope for poems to be written that are worth rubbing over with cedar oil[1] and storing away in cases of polished cypress?

Poets aim at giving either profit or delight, or at combining the giving of pleasure with some useful precepts for life. When you are giving precepts of any kind, be succinct, so that receptive minds may easily grasp what you are saying and retain it firmly; when the mind has plenty to cope with, anything

1. As a preservative.

superfluous merely goes in one ear and out of the other. Works written to give pleasure should be as true to life as possible, and your play should not demand belief for just anything that catches your fancy; you should not let the ogress Lamia gobble up a child, and later bring it out of her belly alive. The centuries of the elder citizens will disapprove of works lacking in edification, while the haughty Ramnes will have nothing to do with plays that are too serious.[1] The man who has managed to blend profit with delight wins everyone's approbation, for he gives his reader pleasure at the same time as he instructs him. This is the book that not only makes money for the booksellers, but is carried to distant lands and ensures a lasting fame for its author.

However, there are faults that we should be ready to forgive; for the lute-string does not always give the note intended by the mind and hand, but often returns a high note when a low one is required, and the bow will not always hit the mark aimed at. When there are plenty of fine passages in a poem, I shall not take exception to occasional blemishes which the poet has carelessly let slip, or which his fallible human nature has not guarded against. What then is our conclusion about this? Just as the literary scribe gets no indulgence if he keeps on making the same mistake however often he is warned, and the lutenist is laughed at if he always goes wrong on the same string, so the poet who is often remiss seems to me another Choerilus,[2] whose two or three good lines I greet with an amused surprise; at the same time I am put out when the worthy Homer nods, although it is natural that slumber should occasionally creep over a long poem.

A poem is like a painting: the closer you stand to this one the more it will impress you, whereas you have to stand a good distance from that one; this one demands a rather dark corner, but that one needs to be seen in full light, and will stand up to the keen-eyed scrutiny of the art-critic; this one only pleased you

1. The Ramnes were one of the three centuries of knights. They seem here to stand, in contrast to the centuries of elders, as representatives of the aristocratic young bloods of the day.

2. Choerilus of Iasos, an inferior epic poet of the time of Alexander the Great. Acron, the commentator on Horace, says that there were only seven good lines in his poem on the exploits of Alexander.

the first time you saw it, but that one will go on giving pleasure however often it is looked at.

A word to you, the elder of the Piso boys. Though you have been trained by your father to form sound judgements and have natural good sense, take this truth to heart and do not forget it: that only in certain walks of life does the second-rate pass muster. An advocate or barrister of mediocre capacity falls short of the eloquent Messalla in ability, and knows less than Aulus Cascellius, yet he is not without his value; on the other hand, neither gods nor men – nor, for that matter, booksellers – can put up with mediocrity in poets. Just as at a pleasant dinner-party music that is out of tune, a coarse perfume, or poppy-seeds served with bitter Sardinian honey give offence, for the meal could just as well have been given without them, so is it with a poem, which is begotten and created for the soul's delight; if it falls short of the top by ever so little, it sinks right down to the bottom. A man who does not understand the games keeps away from the weapons of the Campus Martius, and if he has no skill with the ball or quoit or hoop, he stands quietly aside so that the crowds round the side-lines will not roar with laughter at his expense; yet the man who knows nothing about poetry has the audacity to write it. And why not? he says. He is his own master, a man of good family, and above all he is rated as a knight in wealth and there is nothing against him.

You, I am sure, will not say or do anything counter to the will of Minerva; you have judgement and sense enough for that. But if at any time you do write anything, submit it to the hearing of the critic Maecius, and your father's and mine as well; then put the papers away and keep them for nine years. You can always destroy what you have not published, but once you have let your words go they cannot be taken back.

While men still roamed the forests, they were restrained from bloodshed and a bestial way of life by Orpheus, the sacred prophet and interpreter of the divine will – that is why he is said to have tamed tigers and savage lions. Amphion, too, the founder of Thebes, is credited with having moved stones by the strains of his lyre, and led them where he would with this sweet blandishment. At one time this was the way of the wise man: to distinguish between public and personal rights and between things sacred and profane, to discourage indiscriminate sexual union and make rules for married life, to build towns, and to inscribe laws on tablets of wood. For this reason honour and fame were heaped upon the bards, as divinely inspired beings, and upon their songs. After them the illustrious Homer and Tyrtaeus fired the hearts of men to martial deeds with their verses. In song, too, oracles were delivered, and the way to right living taught; the favour of kings was sought in Pierian strains; and singing-festivals were devised as a close to the year's long toils. So there is no need for you to blush for the Muse, with her skill in song, and for Apollo the god of singers.

The question has been asked whether a fine poem is the product of nature or of art. I myself cannot see the value of application without a strong natural aptitude, or, on the other hand, of native genius unless it is cultivated – so true is it that each requires the help of the other, and that they enter into a friendly compact with each other. The athlete who strains to reach the winning-post has trained hard as a boy and put up with a great deal, sweating, and shivering in the cold, and keeping away from women and wine; the flautist who plays at the Pythian games has first had to learn his art under a stern master. Yet nowadays it is enough for a man to say: 'I write marvellous poems – the devil take the hindmost![1] It would be dreadful if I fell behind and had to admit that I know absolutely nothing about what, after all, I've never learnt.'

Like the auctioneer who gathers a crowd round him anxious to buy his wares, the poet who has plenty of property and plenty of money accumulating interest is a standing invitation to flatterers to swarm round for what they can make out of him. But if he is a man who can put on a first-class dinner in proper style, or stand security for a poor man of little credit, or rescue him when he is tied up in a dismal lawsuit, I shall be surprised if, for all his apparent happiness, he can tell a true friend from a false. And you, if you have given or intend to give anyone a present, do not ask him in the first flush of his delight to listen

1. An allusion to a game like 'Touch me' or tag in which the children cried out, 'The devil take the hindmost.' Horace implies that some people merely play at writing poetry.

to your own poems. 'Lovely!' he will exclaim. 'That's excellent – it's absolutely first-rate!' He will turn quite pale with emotion, and will even be so amiable as to squeeze out a tear or two; he will dance with excitement, or tap out his approval with his foot. Just as at a funeral the paid mourners are on the whole more active and vocal than those who are really suffering deeply, so the mock admirer shows more appreciation than the man who is sincere in his praise. It is said that when kings are anxious to test thoroughly whether a man is worthy of their friendship, they put him to the trial with wine, and ply him with many bumpers. If you are going to write poetry, see to it that you are never put upon by people with the hidden cunning of the fox.

When anything was read to Quintilius Varus, he would say: 'You must put this right – and this too, please.' If after two or three ineffectual attempts you said you could not do any better, he would tell you to get rid of the passage; the lines were badly turned and would have to be hammered out again. If you chose to defend a weakness rather than correct it, he would not say another word, nor waste any effort in trying to prevent you from regarding yourself and your work as unique and unrivalled. An honest, sensible man will condemn any lines that are lifeless, will find fault with them if they are rough, and will run his pen through any that are inelegant; he will cut out any superfluous adornment, will force you to clarify anything that is obscure, and will draw attention to ambiguities; in fact he will prove another Aristarchus and point out everything that requires changing.[1] He will not say, 'Why should I quarrel with a friend over trifles?' Those trifles will bring his friend into serious trouble when once his efforts have been taken amiss and he has become an object of ridicule.

Just as happens when a man is plagued by a nasty rash, or by jaundice, or a fit of lunacy, so men of sense are afraid to have any dealings with a mad poet, and keep clear of him; but children boldly follow him about and tease him. While he is wandering about, spouting his lines with his head in the air like a fowler intent on his game, he can fall into a well or pit, and no one will

1. Aristarchus, an Alexandrian critic of the second century B.C., has been described as 'the greatest critic of antiquity'. His work on the Homeric poems has been the basis of all later texts.

bother to pull him out however long he goes on shouting to the passers-by for help. And if anyone should take the trouble to lend a hand and let down a rope, 'How do you know he didn't jump down there on purpose,' I shall say, 'and doesn't want to be rescued?' and I shall tell the story of the Sicilian poet Empedocles' death. Eager to be regarded as one of the immortal gods, Empedocles in cold blood leapt into the flames of Etna. And poets should have the right to take their own lives. To save a man who does not want to be saved is as good as murdering him. This is not the first time he has tried, and if he is pulled out he will not immediately become a normal human being and abandon his desire to win notoriety by his death. Nor is it very clear why he goes on trying to write poetry – whether because he has defiled his father's ashes, or sacrilegiously violated a place struck by lightning. It is certain, at any rate, that he is raving mad, and like a bear that has been strong enough to burst the bars of its cage, he makes everyone, learned and ignorant alike, take to their heels when he embarks on his detestable recitations. He will fasten on to anyone he manages to catch, and read him to death – just like a leech that will not drop off your skin until it is gorged with blood.

LONGINUS

On the Sublime

LONGINUS
On the Sublime

INTRODUCTION

Cecilius's Treatise and Its Shortcomings

As you will remember, my dear Postumius Terentianus, when we were working together on Cecilius's little treatise on the sublime, it seemed to us too trivial a handling of the subject as a whole; it showed no grasp of the main points, and offered its readers little of the practical help that it should be the writer's main object to supply. In any systematic treatise two things are essential: first, there must be some definition of the subject; second in order of treatment, but of greater importance, there must be some indication of the methods by which we may ourselves reach the desired goal. Now Cecilius, assuming us to be ignorant, sets out to establish the nature of the sublime by means of innumerable examples; but he leaves out of account, apparently considering it unnecessary, the means by which we may be enabled to raise our faculties to the proper pitch of grandeur. However, we ought perhaps rather to praise him for the industry he has shown in carrying out his purpose than find fault with him for his deficiencies.

CHAPTER I

First Thoughts on Sublimity

SINCE you have urged me in my turn to write down my thoughts on the sublime for your gratification, we should consider whether my views contain anything of value to men in public life. And as your nature and your sense of fitness prompt you, my dear friend, you will help me to form the truest possible judgements on the various details; for it was a sound answer that was given by the man who, when asked what we have in common with the gods, replied, 'Benevolence and truth'.

As I am writing for you, Terentianus, who are a man of some erudition, I almost feel that I can dispense with a long preamble showing that sublimity consists in a certain excellence and distinction in expression, and that it is from this source alone that the greatest poets and historians have acquired their pre-eminence and won for themselves an eternity of fame. For the effect of elevated language is, not to persuade the hearers, but to entrance them; and at all times, and in every way, what transports us with wonder is more telling than what merely persuades or gratifies us. The extent to which we can be persuaded is usually under our own control, but these sublime passages exert an irresistible force and mastery, and get the upper hand with every hearer. Inventive skill and the proper order and disposition of material are not manifested in a good touch here and there, but reveal themselves by slow degrees as they run through the whole texture of the composition; on the other hand, a well-timed stroke of sublimity scatters everything before it like a thunderbolt, and in a flash reveals the full power of the speaker. But I should think, my dear Terentianus, that you could develop these points and others of the same kind from your own experience.

CHAPTER 2

Is there an Art of the Sublime?

BEFORE going any farther, I must take up the question whether there is such a thing as an art of sublimity or profundity, for some people think that those who relate matters of this kind to a set of artistic precepts are on a completely wrong track. Genius, they say, is innate; it is not something that can be learnt, and nature is the only art that begets it. Works of natural genius are spoilt, they believe, are indeed utterly debased, when they are reduced to the bare bones of rules and systems. However, I suggest that there is a case for the opposite point of view when it is considered that, although nature is in the main subject only to her own laws where sublime feelings are concerned, she is not given to acting at random and wholly without system. Nature is the first cause and the fundamental creative principle in all activities, but the function of a system is to prescribe the degree and the right moment for each, and to lay down the clearest rules for use and practice. Furthermore, sublime impulses are exposed to greater dangers when they are left to themselves without the ballast and stability of knowledge; they need the curb as often as the spur.

Speaking of the life of mankind as a whole, Demosthenes declares that the greatest of all blessings is good fortune, and that next to it comes good counsel, which, however, is no less important, since its absence leads to the complete destruction of what good fortune brings. Applying this to diction, we might say that nature fills the place of good fortune, and art that of good counsel. Most important, we must remember that the very fact that certain linguistic effects derive from nature alone cannot be learnt from any other source than art. If then the critic who censures those who want to learn this art would take these points into consideration, he would no longer, I imagine, regard the study of the topic I am treating as superfluous and unprofitable.

(Here two pages of the manuscript are missing)

CHAPTER 3

Defects that Militate against Sublimity

... Quell they the oven's far-flung splendour-glow!
Ha, let me but one hearth-abider mark –
One flame-wreath torrent-like I'll whirl on high;
I'll burn the roof, to cinders shrivel it! –
Nay, now my chant is not of noble strain.[1]

SUCH things as this are not tragic, but pseudo-tragic – the 'flame-wreaths', the 'vomiting forth to heaven', the representation of Boreas as a flute-player, and all the rest. They are turbid in expression, and the imagery is confused rather than suggestive of terror; each phrase, when examined in the light of day, sinks gradually from the terrible to the contemptible.

Now even in tragedy, which by its very nature is majestic and admits of some bombast, misplaced tumidity is unpardonable; still less, I think, would it be appropriate to factual narration. This is why people laugh at Gorgias of Leontini[2] when he writes of 'Xerxes the Zeus of the Persians', or of 'vultures, animated sepulchres'. Similarly certain expressions of Callisthenes[3] are ridiculed as being high-flown and not sublime; still more are some of Cleitarchus's[4] – a frivolous fellow who, in the words of Sophocles,[5] blows 'on wretched pipes without control of breath'. Such effects will be found also in Amphicrates and Hegesias and Matris,[6] for often when

1. I have adopted the translation provided by A. S. Way for Roberts's edition, since it brings out so well the bombastic, pseudo-tragic quality to which Longinus takes exception. The lines probably come from a lost *Orithyia* by Aeschylus.

2. A Sicilian rhetorician of the fifth century B.C.

3. A historian who wrote at the end of the fourth and beginning of the third centuries B.C.

4. Another historian, contemporary with Callisthenes; celebrated the deeds of Alexander the Great.

5. The words, probably from a lost *Orithyia* by Sophocles, are quoted in a fuller form by Cicero (*Ad Atticum*).

6. Amphicrates of Athens (*fl.* 90 B.C.), Hegesias of Magnesia (*fl.* 270 B.C.), and Matris of Thebes (*fl.* ? 200 B.C.) were rhetoricians.

they believe themselves to be inspired they are not really carried away, but are merely being puerile.

Tumidity seems, on the whole, to be one of the most difficult faults to guard against. For somehow or other, all those who aim at grandeur in the hope of escaping the charge of feebleness and aridity fall naturally into this very fault, putting their trust in the maxim that 'to fall short of a great aim is at any rate a noble failure'. As in the human body, so also in diction swellings are bad things, mere flabby insincerities that will probably produce an effect opposite to that intended; for as they say, there is nothing drier than a man with dropsy.

Tumidity, then, arises from the desire to outdo the sublime. Puerility, on the other hand, is the complete antithesis of grandeur, for it is entirely low and mean-spirited, and is indeed the most ignoble of faults. What then is puerility? Is it not, surely, a thought which is pedantically elaborated until it tails off into frigidity? Writers slip into this kind of fault when they strive for unusual and well-wrought effects, and above all for attractiveness, and instead flounder into tawdriness and affectation.

Related to this there is a third type of fault in impassioned writing which Theodorus[1] called *parenthyrsus*, or false sentiment. This is misplaced, hollow emotionalism where emotion is not called for, or immoderate passion where restraint is what is needed. For writers are often carried away, as though by drunkenness, into outbursts of emotion which are not relevant to the matter in hand, but are wholly personal, and hence tedious. To hearers unaffected by this emotionalism their work therefore seems atrocious, and naturally enough, for while they are themselves in an ecstasy, their hearers are not. However, I am leaving this matter of the emotions for treatment in another place.

1. Theodorus of Gadara, a rhetorician (*fl.* 30 B.C.).

CHAPTER 4

Frigidity

OF the second fault I mentioned, that is, frigidity, there are plenty of examples in Timaeus,[1] in other respects a writer of some ability, and not incapable of occasional grandeur – a man, indeed, of much learning and inventiveness. However, while he was very fond of criticizing the failings of others, he remained blind to his own, and his passion for continually embarking upon odd conceits often led him into the most trifling puerilities. I shall give you only one or two examples from this author, since Cecilius has anticipated me with most of them. In his eulogy of Alexander the Great he says of him that 'he gained possession of the whole of Asia in fewer years than Isocrates[2] took to write his *Panegyric* advocating war against the Persians.' How remarkable is this comparison of the great Macedonian with the rhetorician! For it is obvious, Timaeus, that, seen in this light, the Spartans were far inferior in prowess to Isocrates, since they took thirty years over the conquest of Messene, whereas he took no more than ten over the composition of his *Panegyric*. Then look at the way in which he speaks of the Athenians captured in Sicily: 'They had behaved sacrilegiously towards Hermes and mutilated statues of him, and it was for this reason that they were punished, very largely through the efforts of a single man, Hermocrates the son of Hermon, who on his father's side was descended from the outraged god.' I am surprised, my dear Terentianus, that he does not write of the tyrant Dionysius that, 'having been guilty of impious conduct towards Zeus and Heracles, he was therefore

1. Timaeus of Tauromenium (*fl.* 310 B.C.), a Sicilian historian who was so fond of finding faults in the work of other writers that he was nicknamed Epitimaeus. i.e., 'fault-finder'.

2. Isocrates (436–338 B.C.), the great Athenian orator and rhetorician. In his *Panegyric* (380 B.C.) he urged the Athenians and the Spartans to lay aside their rivalry and unite against Persia.

deprived of his sovereignty by Dion and Heracleides.'[1]

But why speak of Timaeus when even such demigods as Xenophon and Plato, trained as they were in the school of Socrates, forget themselves at times for the sake of such trivial effects? In his *Constitution of Sparta* Xenophon writes: 'In fact you would hear their voices less than those of marble statues, and would turn aside their gaze less easily than those of bronze figures; and you would think them more modest even than the maidens in their eyes.'[2] It would have been more characteristic of Amphicrates[3] than Xenophon to speak of the pupils of our eyes as modest maidens. And good heavens, to ask us to believe that every single one of them had modest eyes, when it is said that the shamelessness of people is revealed in nothing so much as in their eyes! 'You drunken sot with the eyes of a dog,' as the saying goes.[4] However, Timaeus could not let Xenophon keep even this frigid conceit to himself, but laid his thieving hands on it. At all events, speaking of Agathocles, and how he abducted his cousin from the unveiling ceremony when she had been given in marriage to another man, he asks, 'Who would have done this if he had not had strumpets in his eyes instead of maidens?'

As for the otherwise divine Plato, he says, when he means merely wooden tablets, 'They will inscribe memorials of cypress-wood and place them in the temples;'[5] and again, 'With regard to walls, Megillus, I would agree with Sparta that the walls be allowed to remain lying asleep in the ground, and not rise again.'[6] And Herodotus's phrase for beautiful women, when he calls them 'tortures for the eyes',[7] is not much better. However, Herodotus can in some measure be defended, for it is barbarians who use this phrase in his book, and they in their cups. All the same, it is not proper to put low terms into the

1. The genitive of Zeus is Dios, and Longinus ironically bases on this a conceit in the manner of Timaeus's far-fetched pun on Hermes and Hermocrates the son of Hermon.

2. Because it reflects a tiny image of the person gazing into it, the pupil of the eye was called *korē*, or maiden.

3. An Athenian rhetorician at the beginning of the first century B.C.

4. *Iliad* I, 225.

5. *Laws* V, 741 C.

6. ibid. VI, 778 D.

7. Herodotus, V, 18.

mouths even of such people as these, and thereby lay oneself open to the censure of later ages.

CHAPTER 5

The Origins of Literary Impropriety

ALL these ignoble qualities in literature arise from one cause – from that passion for novel ideas which is the dominant craze among the writers of today; for our faults spring, for the most part, from very much the same sources as our virtues. Thus while a fine style, sublime conceptions, yes, and happy turns of phrase, too, all contribute towards effective composition, yet these very factors are the foundation and origin, not only of success, but also of its opposite. Something of the kind applies also to variations in manner, to hyperbole, and to the idiomatic plural, and I shall show later the dangers which these devices seem to involve. At the moment I must cast about and make some suggestions how we may avoid the defects that are so closely bound up with the achievement of the sublime.

CHAPTER 6

Criticism and the Sublime

THE way to do this, my friend, is first of all to get a clear understanding and appreciation of what constitutes the true sublime. This, however, is no easy undertaking, for the ability to judge literature is the crowning achievement of long experience. Nevertheless, if I am to speak by way of precept, we can perhaps learn discrimination in these matters from some such considerations as those which follow.

CHAPTER 7

The True Sublime

IT must be understood, my dear friend, that, as in everyday life nothing is great which it is considered great to despise, so is it with the sublime. Thus riches, honours, reputation, sovereignty, and all the other things which possess in marked degree the external trappings of a showy splendour, would not seem to a sensible man to be great blessings, since contempt for them is itself regarded as a considerable virtue; and indeed people admire those who possess them less than those who could have them but are high-minded enough to despise them. In the same way we must consider, with regard to the grand style in poetry and literature generally, whether certain passages do not simply give an impression of grandeur by means of much adornment indiscriminately applied, being shown up as mere bombast when these are stripped away – passages which it would be more noble to despise than to admire. For by some innate power the true sublime uplifts our souls; we are filled with a proud exaltation and a sense of vaunting joy, just as though we had ourselves produced what we had heard.

If an intelligent and well-read man can hear a passage several times, and it does not either touch his spirit with a sense of grandeur or leave more food for reflection in his mind than the mere words convey, but with long and careful examination loses more and more of its effectiveness, then it cannot be an example of true sublimity – certainly not unless it can outlive a single hearing. For a piece is truly great only if it can stand up to repeated examination, and if it is difficult, or, rather, impossible to resist its appeal, and it remains firmly and ineffaceably in the memory. As a generalization, you may take it that sublimity in all its truth and beauty exists in such works as please all men at all times. For when men who differ in their pursuits, their ways of life, their ambitions, their ages, and their languages all think in one and the same way about the same works, then the unanimous judgement, as it were, of men who have so little in common induces a strong and unshakeable faith in the object of admiration.

CHAPTER 8

Five Sources of Sublimity

IT may be said that there are five particularly fruitful sources of the grand style, and beneath these five there lies as a common foundation the command of language, without which nothing worth while can be done. The first and most important is the ability to form grand conceptions, as I have explained in my commentary on Xenophon. Second comes the stimulus of powerful and inspired emotion. These two elements of the sublime are very largely innate, while the remainder are the product of art – that is, the proper formation of the two types of figure, figures of thought and figures of speech, together with the creation of a noble diction, which in its turn may be resolved into the choice of words, the use of imagery, and the elaboration of the style. The fifth source of grandeur, which embraces all those I have already mentioned, is the total effect resulting from dignity and elevation.

We must consider, then, what is involved under each of these heads, with a preliminary reminder that Cecilius has left out of account some of the five divisions, one of them obviously being that which relates to emotion. Now if he thought that these two things, sublimity and emotion, were the same thing, and that they were essentially bound up with each other, he is mistaken. For some emotions can be found that are mean and not in the least sublime, such as pity, grief, and fear; and on the other hand many sublime passages convey no emotion, such as, among countless examples, the poet's daring lines about the Aloadae:

> Keenly they strove to set Ossa upon Olympus, and upon Ossa the forest-clad Pelion, that they might mount up to heaven;

and the still greater conception that follows:

> And this would they have accomplished.[1]

With the orators, again, their eulogies, ceremonial addresses,

1. *Odyssey* XI, 315–16; 317.

and occasional speeches contain touches of majesty and grandeur at every point, but as a rule lack emotion; thus emotional speakers are the least effective eulogists, while, on the other hand, those who excel as panegyrists avoid emotionalism. But if Cecilius believed that emotion contributes nothing at all to the sublime, and for this reason considered it not worth mentioning, once again he was making a very serious mistake; for I would confidently maintain that nothing contributes so decisively to the grand style as a noble emotion in the right setting, when it forces its way to the surface in a gust of frenzy, and breathes a kind of divine inspiration into the speaker's words.

CHAPTER 9

Nobility of Soul

Now since the first of these factors, that is to say, nobility of soul,[1] plays the most important part of them all, here too, even though it is a gift rather than an acquired characteristic, we should do all we can to train our minds towards the production of grand ideas, perpetually impregnating them, so to speak, with a noble inspiration. By what means, you will ask, is this to be done? Well, I have written elsewhere to this effect: 'Sublimity is the echo of a noble mind.' Thus, even without being spoken, a simple idea will sometimes of its own accord excite admiration by reason of the greatness of mind that it expresses; for example, the silence of Ajax in 'The Calling Up of the Spirits'[2] is grand, more sublime than any words.

First, then, it is absolutely necessary to indicate the source of this power, and to show that the truly eloquent man must have a mind that is not mean or ignoble. For it is not possible that those who throughout their lives have feeble and servile thoughts and aims should strike out anything that is remarkable, anything that is worthy of an immortality of fame; no,

1. The first of the five sources of sublimity, listed in the previous chapter as 'the ability to form grand conceptions'.

2. *Odyssey* XI, 543 ff.

greatness of speech is the province of those whose thoughts are deep, and stately expressions come naturally to the most high-minded of men. Alexander's reply to Parmenio when he said, 'I would have been content ...'[1]

(*Here six pages of the manuscript are missing*)

... the distance from earth to heaven; and it might be said that this is the stature of Homer as much as of Strife.[2]

Quite different from this is Hesiod's description of Trouble – if indeed *The Shield* is to be ascribed to Hesiod:[3]

> Rheum was running from her nostrils.

The image he has presented is not powerful, but offensive. But see how Homer exalts the heavenly powers:

> And as far as a man can see with his eyes into the hazy distance as he sits upon a mountain-peak and gazes over the wine-dark sea, even so far is the leap of the loudly-neighing steeds of the gods.[4]

He measures their mighty leap in terms of cosmic distances. Might one not exclaim, from the supreme grandeur of this, that if the steeds of the gods make two leaps in succession they will no longer find room on the face of the earth? And vast also are the images he conjures up for the Battle of the Gods:

> And round them rolled the trumpet-tones of the wide heavens and of Olympus. And down in the underworld Hades, monarch of the realm of the shades, leapt from his throne and cried aloud in dread, lest the earth-shaker Poseidon thereafter should cleave the earth apart, and reveal to the gaze of mortals and immortals

1. Arrian (II, 25, 2) records that Parmenio said to Alexander that, if he had been Alexander, he would have been content to end a war on the terms offered without wishing to go further, to which Alexander replied that, if he had been Parmenio, he would have done so.

2. Evidently Longinus has referred to Homer's description of Strife (*Iliad* IV, 442).

3. Hesiod, who belongs probably to the eighth century B.C., is best known for his *Works and Days*. *The Shield of Heracles*, on the authorship of which Longinus casts doubt, is probably the work of an imitator.

4. *Iliad* V, 770 ff.

alike those grim and festering abodes which the very gods look upon with abhorrence.[1]

You see, my friend, how the earth is split from its foundations upwards, how Tartarus itself is laid bare, how the whole universe is turned upside down and torn apart, and everything alike, heaven and hell, things mortal and immortal, shares in the conflict and peril of the combat.

And yet, awe-inspiring as these things are, from another aspect, if they are not taken as allegory, they are altogether ungodly, and do not preserve our sense of what is fitting. In his accounts of the wounds suffered by the gods, their quarrels, their vengeful actions, their tears, their imprisonment, and all their manifold passions, Homer seems to me to have done everything in his power to make gods of the men fighting at Troy, and men of the gods. But while for us mortals, if we are miserable, death is appointed as a refuge from our ills, Homer has given the gods immortality, not only in their nature, but also in their misfortunes.

But far superior to the passages on the Battle of the Gods are those which represent the divine nature as it really is, pure, majestic, and undefiled; for example, the lines on Poseidon, in a passage on which many others before me have commented:

> And the far-stretched mountains and woodlands, and the peaks, and the Trojan city and the ships of the Achaeans trembled beneath the immortal feet of Poseidon as he strode forth. And he went on to drive over the swelling waters, and from all round the monsters of the deep came from their hiding-places and gambolled about him, for they knew their lord. And in rapture the sea parted her waves, and onwards they flew.[2]

So too the lawgiver of the Jews, no ordinary person, having formed a high conception of the power of the Divine Being, gave expression to it when at the very beginning of his Laws he wrote: 'God said' – what? 'Let there be light, and there was light; let there be land, and there was land.'

I should not, I think, seem a bore, my friend, if I were to put before you still one more passage from Homer – one dealing

1. A conflation of *Iliad* XXI, 338 and XX, 61–5.
2. Another conflation: *Iliad* XIII, 18; XX, 60; XIII, 19; 27–9.

with human affairs – in order to show how he habitually associates himself with the sublimity of his heroic themes. All of a sudden the battle of the Greeks is plunged into the impenetrable darkness of night, and then Ajax, utterly at a loss what to do, cries out:

> Father Zeus, do but rescue the sons of Achaea from out of the gloom, give us fair weather, and grant that we may see with our eyes. So long as it be in the light of day, even destroy us.[1]

These are truly the feelings of an Ajax. He does not beg for life, for this plea would be too base for the hero: but since in the crippling darkness he can turn his valour to no noble purpose, he is annoyed that this prevents him from getting on with the fight, and prays for the immediate return of daylight, resolved at least to find a death worthy of his courage, even though Zeus should be fighting against him. Here indeed Homer breathes in the inspiration of the fray, and is affected by it just as if he himself

> is raging madly, like Ares the spear-hurler, or as when ruinous flames rage among the hills, in the thickets of a deep forest, and foam gathers about his lips.[2]

However, throughout the *Odyssey*, which for a number of reasons must be taken into consideration, Homer shows that when a great genius is falling into decline, it is a special mark of his old age that he should be fond of fables. For it is clear on many grounds that he produced this work as his second composition, besides the fact that throughout the *Odyssey* he introduces remnants of the experiences at Troy as episodes from the Trojan War. And indeed he there pays a debt of mourning and lamentation to his heroes as something long due to them. In fact the *Odyssey* is nothing more than an epilogue to the *Iliad*:

> There lies Ajax the great warrior, there Achilles, there too Patroclus, peer of the gods in counsel; and there too my own dear son.[3]

1. *Iliad* XVII, 645–7.
2. *Iliad* XV, 605–7.
3. *Odyssey* III, 109–11. Nestor is telling Telemachus about the siege of Troy.

It was, I suppose, for the same reason that, writing the *Iliad* in the prime of life, he filled the whole work with action and conflict, whereas the greater part of the *Odyssey* is narrative, as is characteristic of old age. Thus in the *Odyssey* Homer may be likened to the setting sun, whose grandeur remains without its intensity; for no longer there does he maintain the same pitch as in those lays of Troy. The sublime passages have not that consistency which nowhere lapses into mediocrity, nor is there the same closely-packed profusion of passions, nor the versatile and oratorical style studded with images drawn from real life. As though the ocean were withdrawing into itself and remaining quietly within its own bounds, from now on we see the ebbing of Homer's greatness as he wanders in the realms of the fabulous and the incredible. In saying this I have not forgotten the storms in the *Odyssey* and the episode of the Cyclops and other things of the kind. I am speaking indeed of old age, but after all it is the old age of a Homer. Nevertheless, in every one of these passages the fabulous predominates over the actual.

As I said, I have digressed in this way in order to show how very easily a great spirit in his decline may at times be misled into writing nonsense; examples are the episodes of the wine-skin,[1] of the men whom Circe fed like swine, and whom Zoilus[2] described as 'wailing piglets', of Zeus nurtured by the doves like a nestling, and of the man remaining without food on the wreck for ten days,[3] and the incredible story of the killing of the suitors. For how else are we to describe these things than as veritable dreams of Zeus?

There is another reason why these comments should be made on the *Odyssey*, and that is that you should understand how the decline of emotional powers in poets and prose-writers leads to the study of character. For of this kind are the facts, given from the point of view of character, of the way of life in Odysseus's household; they constitute what is in effect a comedy of character.

1. *Odyssey* X, 17. The wine-skin in which Aeolus enclosed for Odysseus the unfavourable winds, which were released by his followers.

2. A grammarian and critic of the fourth century B.C. who was nick-named 'Homer's Scourge' for his carping criticism of Homer.

3. A reference to Odysseus's ten-day swim at the end of *Odyssey* XII.

CHAPTER 10

The Selection and Organization of Material

NEXT we must consider whether there is anything else that makes for sublimity of style. Now as we naturally associate with all things certain elements that are inherent in their substance, so it necessarily follows that we shall find one source of the sublime in the unerring choice of the most felicitous of these elements, and in the ability to relate them to one another in such a way as to make of them a single organism, so to speak. For one writer attracts the hearer by his choice of matter, another by the cumulative effect of the ideas he chooses. For example, Sappho in her poetry always chooses the emotions attendant on the lover's frenzy from among those which accompany this passion in real life. And wherein does she demonstrate her excellence? In the skill with which she selects and fuses the most extreme and intense manifestations of these emotions:

> A peer of the gods he seems to me, the man who sits over against you face to face, listening to the sweet tones of your voice and the loveliness of your laughing; it is this that sets my heart fluttering in my breast. For if I gaze on you but for a little while, I am no longer master of my voice, and my tongue lies useless, and a delicate flame runs over my skin. No more do I see with my eyes, and my ears are filled with uproar. The sweat pours down me, I am all seized with trembling, and I grow paler than the grass. My strength fails me, and I seem little short of dying.[1]

Are you not astonished at the way in which, as though they were gone from her and belonged to another, she at one and the same time calls up soul and body, ears, tongue, eyes, and colour; how, uniting opposites, she freezes while she burns, is both out of her senses and in her right mind? For she is either terrified or not far from dying. And all this is done so that not

1. This ode of Sappho (born about the middle of the seventh century B.C.) is traditionally regarded as a farewell song written for one of her favourite pupils, Anactoria. Imitation of the ode occurs in Catullus, *Carmina* LI.

one emotion alone may be seen in her, but a concourse of emotions. All such emotions as these are awakened in lovers, but it is, as I said, the selection of them in their most extreme forms and their fusion into a single whole that have given the poem its distinction.

In the same way Homer in describing storms singles out their most terrifying properties. The author of the *Arimaspeia*[1] thinks the following passage to be awe-inspiring:

> This also to our minds is a great marvel. There are men dwelling in the waters of the ocean, far away from land. Wretched creatures they are, for grievous is the trouble they undergo, fixing their gaze upon the stars and their spirit upon the waters. Often, methinks, they lift up their hands to the gods, and with their hearts raised heavenwards they pray in their misery.

It is obvious to anyone, I imagine, that this passage is more flowery than terrifying. But how does Homer set about it? Let us choose one out of many possible examples:

> And he fell upon them like a wave which, swollen by the stormwinds beneath the lowering clouds, bursts furiously over a hurrying ship. And the ship is all lost in foam, and the terrifying blast roars in the sail, and the souls of the crew are seized with a fearful shuddering, for barely can they slip out from under the clutch of death.[2]

Aratus made an attempt to adapt this same idea to his own purposes:

> And a slender plank wards off destruction.[3]

However, he has made it trivial and elegant instead of terrifying. Furthermore, by saying that a plank keeps away destruction, he has kept the danger within bounds – after all, the plank does keep it away. On the other hand, Homer does not for a moment limit the terror, but draws a picture of his sailors again and again, all the time, on the brink of destruction with the coming of each wave. Moreover, in 'out from under the clutch of

1. Aristeas of Proconnesus (*fl.* 580 B.C.) wrote an epic in three books on the Arimaspi, the dwellers of the far north.

2. *Odyssey* XV, 624–8.

3. Line 299 of the *Phaenomena* of Aratus, an Alexandrian poet writing in the first half of the third century B.C.

death' he has exerted an abnormal force in thrusting together prepositions not usually compounded, and has thus twisted his language to bring it into conformity with the impending disaster; and by this compressed language he has supremely well pictured the disaster and all but stamped on the diction the very image of the danger – 'slip out from under the clutch of death'. Not dissimilar are the passage of Archilochus[1] relating to the shipwreck, and that in which Demosthenes, describing the bringing of the news, begins, 'For it was evening ...'.[2] It might be said that these writers have brought out the striking points in order of merit and massed them together, finding no place among them for anything frivolous, undignified, or long-winded. For such faults as these ruin the total effect of a passage, like air-holes and other orifices foisted on to impressive and harmonious buildings whose walls are ordered into a coherent structure.[3]

CHAPTER 11

Amplification

A MERIT associated with those already presented is that which is called amplification, that is, when the matters under discussion or the points of an argument allow of many pauses and many fresh starts from section to section, and the grand phrases come rolling out one after another with increasing effect.

This may be managed either by the rhetorical development of a commonplace, or by exaggeration, whether facts or arguments are to be stressed, or by the orderly disposition of factual points or of appeals to the feelings. There are, indeed, countless forms of amplification. Yet the speaker must be aware that, without the help of sublimity, none of these methods can of itself form a complete whole, unless indeed in the expression of pity or

1. Archilochus of Paros (*fl.* 650 B.C.).
2. Demosthenes, *De Corona*, 169.
3. This sentence is about the best that can be made of a corrupt passage which has been variously emended.

disparagement. In other forms of amplification, when you take away the element of the sublime, it will be like taking the soul out of the body; for their vigour will be completely drained away without the sustaining power of the sublime.

However, in the interests of clarity I must briefly indicate how my present precepts differ from those about which I have just spoken, that is, the marking-out of the most striking points and their organization into a single whole, and in what general respects sublimity is to be distinguished from the effects of amplification.

CHAPTER 12

Amplification Defined

Now the definition of the writers on rhetoric is not, in my view, acceptable. Amplification, they say, is language which invests the subject with grandeur. But obviously this definition could apply equally well to sublimity and to the emotional and the figurative styles, since these too invest language with some degree of grandeur. As I see it, they are to be distinguished from one another by the fact that sublimity consists in elevation, amplification in quantity; thus sublimity is often contained in a single idea, whereas amplification is always associated with quantity and a certain amount of redundancy. To sum it up in general terms, amplification is the accumulation of all the small points and incidental topics bearing on the subject-matter; it adds substance and strength to the argument by dwelling on it, differing from proof in that, while the latter demonstrates the point at issue . . .

(*Here two pages of the manuscript are lost*)

. . . extremely rich; like some ocean, he[1] often swells into a mighty expanse of grandeur. From this I should say that, where language is concerned, the orator,[2] being more concerned with the emotions, shows much fire and vehemence of spirit, whilst

1. Chapter 13 makes it clear that this refers to Plato.
2. Demosthenes.

Plato, standing firmly based upon his supreme dignity and majesty, though indeed he is not cold, has not the same vehemence.

It seems to me that it is on these same grounds, my dear Terentianus – if we Greeks may be allowed an opinion in this matter – that Cicero is to be differentiated from Demosthenes in his use of the grand style. Demosthenes is characterized by a sublimity which is for the most part rugged, Cicero by profusion. Demosthenes, by reason of his force, yes, and his speed and power and intensity, may be likened to a thunderbolt or flash of lightning, as it were burning up or seizing as his own all that he falls upon. But Cicero is, in my opinion, like a wide-spreading conflagration that rolls on to consume everything far and wide; he has within him an abundance of steady and enduring flame which can be let loose at whatever point he desires, and which is fed from one source after another.

However, you Romans should be able to form a better judgement in this matter. But the right place for the Demosthenean sublimity and intensity is in passages where hyperbole and powerful emotions are involved, and where the audience are to be swept off their feet. On the other hand, profusion is in order when it is necessary to flood them with words. It is for the most part appropriate to the treatment of rhetorical commonplaces, and of perorations and digressions; well suited, too, to all descriptive and epideictic[1] writings, to works of history and natural philosophy, and to a number of other types of literature.

CHAPTER 13

Plato and the Sublime. Imitation

Now although Plato – for I must return to him – flows with such a noiseless stream, he none the less achieves grandeur. You are familiar with his *Republic* and know his manner. 'Those,

1. Epideictic orations were one of the types of set speech defined in the rhetorical systems of the ancients – in Latin *genus demonstrativum*; they include such things as funeral orations, panegyrics, and speeches of dispraise.

therefore,' he says,[1] 'who have no experience of wisdom and goodness, and are always engaged in feasting and similar pleasures, are brought down, it would seem, to a lower level, and there wander about all their lives. They have never looked up towards the truth, nor risen higher, nor tasted of any pure and lasting pleasure. In the manner of cattle, they bend down with their gaze fixed always on the ground and on their feeding-places, grazing and fattening and copulating, and in their insatiable greed for these pleasures they kick and butt one another with horns and hoofs of iron, and kill one another if their desires are not satisfied.'

Provided that we are ready to give him due attention, this author shows us that, in addition to those already mentioned, there is another way that leads to the sublime. And what kind of a way is this? It is the imitation and emulation of the great historians and poets of the past. Let us steadfastly keep this aim in mind, my dear fellow. For many authors catch fire from the inspiration of others – just as we are told that the Pythian priestess, when she approaches the tripod standing by a cleft in the ground from which, they say, there is breathed out a divine vapour, is impregnated thence with the heavenly power, and by virtue of this afflatus is at once inspired to speak oracles. So too, as though also issuing from sacred orifices, certain emanations are conveyed from the genius of the men of old into the souls of those who emulate them, and, breathing in these influences, even those who show very few signs of inspiration derive some degree of divine enthusiasm from the grandeur of their predecessors.

Was Herodotus alone an extremely Homeric writer? No, for even earlier there was Stesichorus,[2] and Archilochus, and above all others Plato, who for his own use drew upon countless tributary streams from the great Homeric river. I should perhaps have had to prove this had not Ammonius[3] and his followers selected and recorded the facts.

1. *Republic* IX, 586.
2. Stesichorus (*c.* 640 – *c.* 555 B.C.), one of the great lyrical poets.
3. Ammonius (*fl.* 140 B.C.) carried on at Alexandria the work of his master Aristarchus, who has been described as 'the founder of scientific scholarship'.

Now this procedure is not plagiarism; rather it is like taking impressions from beautiful pictures or statues or other works of art. I do not think there would have been so fine a bloom on Plato's philosophical doctrines, or that he would so often have embarked on poetic subject-matter and phraseology, had he not been striving heart and soul with Homer for first place, like a young contestant entering the ring with a long-admired champion, perhaps showing too keen a spirit of emulation in his desire to break a lance with him, so to speak, yet getting some profit from the endeavour. For as Hesiod says,[1] 'This strife is good for mortals.' And indeed the fight for fame and the crown of victory are noble and very well worth the winning where even to be worsted by one's predecessors carries no discredit.

CHAPTER 14

Some Practical Advice

It is well, then, that we too, when we are working at something that demands grandeur both of conception and of expression, should carefully consider how perhaps Homer might have said this very thing, or how Plato, or Demosthenes, or Thucydides in his History, might have given it sublimity. For conjured up before our eyes, as it were, by our spirit of emulation, these great men will raise our minds to the standards we have laid down for ourselves.

Still more will this be so if we put to ourselves the further query, 'How would Homer or Demosthenes, if he had been present, have listened to this passage of mine, and how would it have affected him?' For indeed it would be a severe ordeal to bring our own utterances before such a court of justice and such a theatre as this, to make a pretence of submitting our writings to the scrutiny of such semi-divine judges and witnesses.

It would be even more stimulating if you added the question, 'What kind of hearing should I get from all future ages if I

1. *Works and Days* 24.

wrote this?' But if anyone shrinks from the expression of anything beyond the comprehension of his own time and age, the conceptions of his mind are obviously obscure and incomplete, and are bound to come to nothing, since they are by no means brought to such perfection as to ensure their fame in later ages.

CHAPTER 15

Imagery and the Power of the Imagination

FURTHERMORE, my dear boy, dignity, grandeur, and powers of persuasion are to a very large degree derived from images – for that is what some people call the representation of mental pictures. In a general way the term 'image' is used of any mental conception, from whatever source it presents itself, which gives rise to speech; but in current usage the word is applied to passages in which, carried away by your feelings, you imagine you are actually seeing the subject of your description, and enable your audience as well to see it. You will have noticed that imagery means one thing with orators and another with poets – that in poetry its aim is to work on the feelings, in oratory to produce vividness of description, though indeed in both cases an attempt is made to stir the feelings.

> Mother, I beseech you, do not set upon me those blood-boltered and snake-like hags. See there, see there, they approach, they leap upon me![1]

and again,

> Ah! She will slay me! Whither shall I fly?[2]

In these passages the poet himself had 'seen' the Furies, and he almost compelled his audience, too, to see what he had imagined.

Now Euripides expends his highest powers in giving tragic expression to these two passions, madness and love, and he is more brilliantly successful with these, I think, than with any others, although he is not afraid to make incursions into other

1. Euripides, *Orestes* 255–7.
2. Euripides, *Iphigenia in Tauris* 291.

realms of the imagination. While he is very far from possessing a natural grandeur, yet on many occasions he forces his genius to tragic heights, and where sublimity is concerned, each time, in the words of Homer,

> with his tail he lashes his ribs and flanks on both sides, and goads himself on to fight.[1]

For example, when the Sun hands the reins to Phaethon, he says:

> 'And do not as you drive venture into the Libyan sky, for being tempered with no moisture it will burn up your wheel.'[2]

And he goes on,

> 'But speed your course towards the seven Pleiades.' And hearing this, the boy took hold of the reins, and lashed the flanks of his winged team, and they winged their path up to the cloudy ridges of the sky. And hard behind rode his father, astride the Dog-Star's back, schooling his son: 'Drive that way! Now this way guide the chariot, this way!'

Now would you not say that the soul of the poet goes into the chariot with the boy, sharing his danger and joining the horses in their flight? For he could never have formed such an image had he not been swept along neck by neck with these celestial activities. You will find the same in the words he gives to Cassandra:

> Yet, you Trojans, lovers of steeds . . .[3]

Aeschylus, too, ventures on images of a most heroic cast, as when he says in his *Seven against Thebes*:

> Seven resistless warrior-captains have slit a bullock's throat over an iron-rimmed shield, and have brushed their hands over the bullock's blood and sworn an oath by War and Havoc and Terror, the lover of blood . . .[4]

1. *Iliad* XX, 170–1.
2. This and the following passage are taken from the lost *Phaethon* of Euripides.
3. From another lost play of Euripides.
4. *Seven against Thebes*, 42–6.

Here they pledge themselves by a joint oath to a pitiless death. Sometimes, however, Aeschylus introduces ideas that are unfinished and crude and harsh; yet Euripides in a desire to emulate him comes dangerously near to committing the same faults. For example, in Aeschylus the palace of Lycurgus at the appearance of Dionysus is described in unusual terms as being divinely possessed:

> Then the house is in an ecstasy, and the roof is inspired with a Bacchic frenzy.[1]

Euripides has expressed the same idea differently, softening it down:

> And the whole mountain joined with them in their Bacchic frenzy.[2]

Sophocles, too, has used excellent imagery in describing the death of Oedipus as he entombs himself amid portents from the sky,[3] and in his account of how, at the departure of the Greeks, Achilles shows himself above his tomb to those who are sailing away,[4] a scene which I think no one has depicted more vividly than Simonides.

But it would be out of the question to quote all the examples. However, as I have said, those from the poets display a good deal of romantic exaggeration, and everywhere exceed the bounds of credibility, whereas the finest feature of the orator's imagery is always its adherence to reality and truth. Whenever the texture of the speech becomes poetical and fabulous, and falls into all sorts of impossibilities, such deviations seem strange and unnatural. Our brilliant modern orators, for example, see Furies, heaven help us, just as though they were tragedians, and, noble fellows that they are, they cannot even understand that when Orestes says,

> Be off, for you are one of my avenging Furies clasping my waist to hurl me down to hell,[5]

he is imagining this because he is mad.

1. From a lost play of Aeschylus.
2. Euripides, *Bacchae* 726.
3. Sophocles, *Oedipus at Colonus* 1,586–666.
4. In his lost *Polyxena*. The poem in which Simonides describes the same episode is also lost.
5. Euripides, *Orestes* 264–5.

What, then, is the effect of imagery when it is used in oratory? Among other things, it can infuse much passion and energy into speeches, but when it is combined with the argumentative passages it not only persuades the hearer, but actually masters him.

'Suppose,' says Demosthenes,[1] to give an example, 'suppose that at this very moment an uproar were to be heard in front of the courts, and someone were to tell us that the prison had been broken open and the prisoners were escaping, there is no one, old or young, so irresponsible that he would not give all the help in his power; moreover, if someone were to come and tell us that so-and-so was the person who let them out, he would at once be put to death without a hearing.' Then of course there is Hyperides,[2] who was put on trial when he had proposed the enfranchisement of the slaves after the great defeat; his answer was that it was not himself, the advocate, who had framed the measure, but the battle of Chaeronea. Here the orator has at one and the same time developed an argument and used his imagination, and his conception has therefore transcended the bounds of mere persuasion. In all such cases our ears always, by some natural law, seize upon the stronger element, so that we are attracted away from the demonstration of fact to the startling image, and the argument lies below the surface of the accompanying brilliance. And it is not unreasonable that we should be affected in this way, for when two forces are combined to produce a single effect, the greater always attracts to itself the virtues of the lesser.

I have gone far enough in my discussion of sublimity of thought, as it is produced by greatness of mind, imitation, or imagery.

1. Demosthenes, *Timocrates* 208.

2. Hyperides (389–22 B.C.), a distinguished Attic orator. See Chapter 34. Plutarch relates (*Moralia* 849 A) that after the Athenian defeat at Chaeronea Hyperides proposed an extension of the franchise, and, when he was impeached for the illegality of his proposal, declared, 'The arms of the Macedonians obscured my vision; it was not I who proposed the measure, but the battle of Chaeronea.'

CHAPTER 16

Rhetorical Figures: Adjuration

We now come to the place which I have duly set aside for rhetorical figures, for they too, when properly handled, will contribute in no small measure, as I have said, to the effect of grandeur. However, since it would be a toilsome and indeed endless business to consider them all closely at this stage, I shall merely, in order to confirm my proposition, run over a few of those which make for grandeur of utterance.

In the following passage Demosthenes is putting forward an argument in support of his policy. What was the natural procedure for doing this? 'You were not wrong, you who undertook the struggle for the freedom of the Greeks, and you have a precedent for this here at home. For those who fought at Marathon were not wrong, nor those at Salamis, nor those at Plataea.'[1] But when, as though carried away by a divine enthusiasm and by the inspiration of Phoebus himself, he uttered his oath by the champions of Greece, 'By those who stood the shock at Marathon, it cannot be that you were wrong,' it would seem that, by his use of this single figure of adjuration, which I here give the name of apostrophe, he has deified his ancestors by suggesting that we ought to swear by men who have died such deaths as we swear by gods; he has instilled into his judges the spirit of the men who stood there in the forefront of the danger, and has transformed the natural flow of his argument into a passage of transcending sublimity, endowing it with the passion and the power of conviction that arise from unheard-of and extraordinary oaths. At the same time he has infused into the minds of his audience words which act in some sort as an antidote and a remedy, so that, uplifted by these eulogies, they come to feel just as proud of the war against Philip as of the triumphs at Marathon and Salamis. By all these

1. *De Corona* 208. Demosthenes is defending, by reference to the past, his aggressive policy which resulted in the Athenian defeat at Chaeronea.

means he has been able to carry his hearers away with the figure he has employed.

It is said, indeed, that Demosthenes found the germ of this oath in Eupolis:[1]

> For by the fight I fought at Marathon, no one of them shall vex my heart and not pay for it.

But there is nothing grand about the mere swearing of an oath; we must take into account the place, the manner, the circumstances, and the motive. In the Eupolis there is nothing but an oath, and that addressed to the Athenians while they were still enjoying prosperity and in no need of consolation. Moreover, the poet has not in his oath deified the warriors in order to engender in his audience a high opinion of their valour, but has wandered away from those who stood the shock to something inanimate, that is, the fight. In Demosthenes the oath is designed for men who have suffered defeat, so that the Athenians may no longer regard Chaeronea as a disaster; and at the same time it is, as I said, a proof that no wrong has been done, an example, a demonstration of the efficacy of oaths, a eulogy, and an exhortation. And since the orator was likely to be faced with the objection, 'You are speaking of a defeat that resulted from your policy, yet your oath relates to victories,' in what follows he keeps on the safe side and measures every word, showing that even in orgies of the imagination it is necessary to remain sober. 'Those who stood in the forefront of the battle at Marathon,' he says, 'and those who fought aboard ship at Salamis and Artemisium, and those who stood shoulder to shoulder at Plataea.' Nowhere does he speak of the 'victors'; everywhere he cunningly avoids mention of the result, since it was a happy one and the reverse of what happened at Chaeronea. Thus he anticipates objections and carries his audience with him. 'To all of whom, Aeschines,' he adds, 'the state gave a public funeral, not only to those who were successful.'

1. Eupolis (*c.* 446 – *c.* 411 B.C.) was a poet of the Old Comedy. The lines come from his lost comedy *Demi*.

CHAPTER 17

Rhetorical Figures and Sublimity

IN this matter, my dear friend, I must not omit an observation of my own, which, however, shall be quite concisely stated. This is that, by some quality innate in them, the rhetorical figures reinforce the sublime, and in their turn derive a marvellous degree of support from it. I will tell you where and how this happens. The unconscionable use of figures is peculiarly subject to suspicion, and engenders impressions of hidden traps and plots and fallacies. This is true when the speech is addressed to a judge with absolute authority, and still more to despots, kings, or rulers in high places, for such a one is at once annoyed if, like a simple child, he is caught on the wrong foot by the rhetorical devices of a highly-skilled orator. Accepting the fallacy as a personal insult, he sometimes turns quite savage, and even if he masters his rage, he becomes utterly impervious to the persuasive quality of the speech. Thus a rhetorical figure would appear to be most effective when the fact that it is a figure is not apparent.

Sublimity and the expression of strong feeling are, therefore, a wonderfully helpful antidote against the suspicion that attends the use of figures. The cunning artifice remains out of sight, associated from now on with beauty and sublimity, and all suspicion is put to flight. Sufficient evidence of this is the passage already mentioned, 'I swear by the men of Marathon!' But by what means has the orator here concealed his figure? Obviously by its very brilliance. For in much the same way as dim lights vanish in the radiance of the sun, so does the all-pervading effluence of grandeur utterly obscure the artifices of rhetoric.

Something of the same kind occurs also in painting. For although light and shade as represented by colours may lie side by side on the same surface, it is the light that first catches the eye and seems not only to stand out, but also to be much nearer. So also is it with literature: by some natural affinity and by their brilliance, things that appeal to our feelings and sublime conceptions lie nearer to our hearts, and always catch our attention before the figures, overshadowing their artistry, and keeping it out of sight, so to speak.

CHAPTER 18

Rhetorical Questions

BUT what are we to say on the matter of questions and answers? Does not Demosthenes aim at enhancing the grandeur and effectiveness of his speeches very considerably by the very way in which he exploits these figures and their appeal to the imagination? 'Now tell me, do you want to go about asking one another, "Is there any news?"? For what stranger news could there be than that of a Macedonian conquering Greece? "Is Philip dead?" "No, but he is ill." What difference does it make to you? For even if anything should happen to him, you will soon invent another Philip.'[1] And again, 'Let us sail against Macedonia,' he says. '"But where shall we land?" someone asks. The mere fact of our fighting will find out the weak spots in Philip's strategy.'[2] If this had been given as a bald statement, it would have been completely ineffective; but as it is, the inspired rapidity in the play of question and answer, together with the device of meeting his own objections as though they were someone else's, has not only added to the sublimity of his words, but also given them greater conviction, and all this by the use of this particular figure. For a display of feeling is more effective when it seems not to be premeditated on the part of the speaker, but to have arisen from the occasion; and this method of asking questions and providing your own answers gives the appearance of being a natural outburst of feeling. Those who are being questioned by others are stimulated into answering the questions spontaneously, and with energy and complete candour; in the same way the rhetorical figure of question and answer beguiles the audience into thinking that

1. Demosthenes, *Philippic* I, 10.
2. ibid. 44.

each deliberately considered point has been struck out and put into words on the spur of the moment. Furthermore – for the following passage has been accepted as one of the most sublime in Herodotus – if thus . . .

(Here two pages of the manuscript are missing)

CHAPTER 19

Asyndeton, or the Omission of Conjunctions

. . . the words come gushing out, as it were, set down without connecting links, and almost outstripping the speaker himself. 'And, locking their shields,' says Xenophon,[1] 'they pressed forward, fought, slew, were slain.' Then there are the words of Eurylochus:

> We came through the oak-coppice, as you bade, renowned Odysseus. We saw amid the forest-glens a beautiful palace.[2]

The phrases, disconnected, but none the less rapid, give the impression of an agitation which at the same time checks the utterance and urges it on. And the poet has produced such an effect by his use of asyndeton.

CHAPTER 20

The Accumulation of Figures

A COMBINATION of figures for a common purpose usually has a very moving effect – when two or three unite in a kind of partnership to add force, persuasiveness, and beauty. Thus in Demosthenes' speech against Meidias you will find examples of asyndeton interwoven with the figures of anaphora and diatyposis:[3] 'For the aggressor might do many things, some

1. Xenophon, *Historia Graeca* IV, 3, 19.
2. *Odyssey* X, 251–2.
3. Anaphora is the repetition of words; diatyposis is vivid description.

of which the victim would be unable to describe to anyone else, by his manner, his looks, his voice.' Then, in order that the speech may not, as it proceeds, remain at a standstill as far as these particular effects are concerned (for standing still connotes calm, whereas emotion, being an upheaval or agitation of the soul, connotes disorder), he at once hurries on to fresh examples of asyndeton and anaphora: 'By his manner, his looks, his voice, when he acts with insolence, when he acts with hostility, when he strikes you with his fists, when he strikes you like a slave.' In this way the orator does just the same as the aggressor; he belabours the judges' minds with blow after blow. He goes on from here to make yet another hurricane onslaught: 'When he strikes you with his fists,' he says, 'when he beats you about the face – this rouses you, this drives men out of their wits when they are not used to being trampled underfoot. No one describing this could bring out the strength of its effect.' Thus all the way through, although with continual variations, he preserves the essential character of the repetitions and the asyndeta, and thus too his order is disordered, and similarly his disorder embraces a certain element of order.

CHAPTER 21

Conjunctions: Some Disadvantages

Now, if you will, try putting in the conjunctions, in the manner of Isocrates[1] and his disciples: 'Furthermore, this too must not be overlooked, that the aggressor might do many things, first by his manner, then by his looks, and then again by his mere voice.' If you amplify it like this, phrase by phrase, you will see that the drive and ruggedness of the emotion that is being exploited, toned down into smoothness by the use of the conjunctions, lapse into pointlessness and at once lose all their fire. If you tie runners together you will deprive them of their speed; in exactly the same way emotion resents being hampered

1. Isocrates (436–338 B.C.), a great Athenian orator. His disciples included Hyperides (see Chapters 15 and 34) and Theopompus (see Chapters 31 and 43).

by conjunctions and other appendages of the kind, for it then loses its freedom of motion and the impression it gives of being shot from a catapult.

CHAPTER 22

The Figure of Hyperbaton, or Inversion

HYPERBATA, or inversions, must be put into the same class. These consist in the arrangement of words or ideas out of their normal sequence, and they carry, so to speak, the genuine stamp of powerful emotion. There are people who, when they are angry or frightened or irritated or carried away by jealousy or any other feeling – for there are innumerable forms of emotion, and indeed no one would be able to say just how many – will sometimes let themselves be deflected; and often, after they have brought forward one point, they will drop in others without rhyme or reason, and then, under the stress of their agitation, they will come right round to their original position just as though they were being chased by a whirlwind. Dragged in every direction by their rapid changes of mood, they will keep altering the arrangement of their words and ideas, losing their natural sequence and introducing all sorts of variations. In the same way the best authors will use inversion in such a way that their representations will assume the aspect of natural processes at work. For art is perfect only when it looks like nature, and again, nature hits the mark only when she conceals the art that is within her.

This may be exemplified by the words of Dionysius the Phocaean in Herodotus:[1] 'For our affairs stand on a razor's edge, men of Ionia, whether we are to be free men or slaves, and runaway slaves at that. Now, therefore, if you are prepared to accept hardships, straightway there is toil for you, but you will be able to overcome your enemies.' Here the normal order would have been, 'O men of Ionia, now is the time for you to take toil upon you; for our affairs stand on a razor's edge.' However, the speaker has transposed 'men of Ionia', starting at

1. Herodotus, VI, 11.

once with the thought of the fear, as though in this pressing danger he would not even address his hearers first. Furthermore, he has inverted the order of his ideas; for instead of saying that they must endure toil ,which is the point of his exhortation, he first gives them the reason why they must toil when he says, 'Our affairs stand on a razor's edge.' Thus what he says does not seem premeditated, but forced out of him.

Thucydides is even more skilful in his use of inversions to dissociate things which are by their nature one and indivisible. Demosthenes, though indeed he is not as wilful as Thucydides, is the most immoderate of all in his use of this kind of figure, and through inversions he gives the impression of speaking extremely masterfully, and, what is more, of speaking impromptu; moreover, he carries his audience with him to share in the dangers of his long inversions. For he will often hold up the sense of what he has begun to express, and meanwhile he will in a strange and unlikely order pile one idea on top of another, drawn from any kind of source and just dropped into the middle of what he is saying, inducing in his hearer the fear that the whole structure of the sentence will fall to pieces, and compelling him in his agitation to share in the risk the speaker is taking; and then unexpectedly, after a long interval, he will bring out the long-awaited phrase just where it is most effective, at the very end, and thus, by the very audacity and recklessness of his inversions, he administers a much more powerful shock. I forbear to give examples, since there are so many of them.

CHAPTER 23

Polyptoton: Interchange of Singular and Plural

THE figures called polyptota[1] (accumulations, variations, and climaxes) are, as you know, very powerful auxiliaries in the production of elegance and of every kind of sublime and emotional effect. Observe, too, how greatly an exposition is

1. Strictly speaking, polyptoton is the use of more than one case of the same word, but Longinus seems to apply it also to rhetorical effects gained by changes in number, person, tense, or gender.

diversified and enlivened by changes in case, tense, person, number, and gender. In the matter of number, I can say that the decorative quality of a passage is not enhanced only by words which are singular in form, but which on close examination are found to have a plural meaning, as in

> Straightway a countless host ranged along the beaches send out a cry, 'Tunny!'[1]

But it is more noteworthy that at times the use of the plural in place of the singular has a more resounding effect, and impresses us by the very idea of multitude implied in the plural number. This is exemplified by Sophocles in some lines spoken by Oedipus:

> O marriages, marriages, it is you that begot me and gave me birth, and then brought to light again the same seed, and showed fathers, brothers, and sons as being all kindred blood, and brides, wives, and mothers, too, and all the foulest deeds that are done among men.[2]

All these relate to a single name, that of Oedipus, with that of Jocasta on the other side; however, the expansion of the number serves to pluralize the misfortunes as well.

There is the same kind of multiplication in the line, 'Forth came Hectors, and Sarpedons too;'[3] and again in Plato's passage on the Athenians which I have also quoted in another work: 'For no Pelopes nor Cadmi nor Aegypti and Danai, nor any other hordes of barbarians by birth share our home with us, but we who are pure Greeks and not semi-barbarians live here', and the rest of it.[4] For naturally the facts sound more impressive from this accumulation of names in groups. However, this should not be done except on occasions when the subject admits of amplification or redundancy or exaggeration or emotionalism – any one or more of these; for to be hung all over with bells is altogether too pretentious.[5]

1. Author unknown. Presumably the passage refers to a crowd of fisherfolk hailing the appearance of a shoal of tunny.

2. *Oedipus Tyrannus* 1403–8.

3. Author unknown.

4. Plato, *Menexenus* 245 D.

5. The metaphor here refers to the bells hung on the trappings of a war-horse. Roberts translates, 'a richly caparisoned style'.

CHAPTER 24

Polyptoton: Conversion of Plural to Singular

FURTHERMORE, the opposite process, the contraction of plural ideas into a singular form, sometimes achieves an outstanding effect of sublimity. 'Afterwards,' says Demosthenes,[1] 'the whole Peloponnese was at variance.' Again, 'And when Phrynicus produced his play *The Capture of Miletus* the theatre burst into tears.'[2] To compress the number from multiplicity into unity gives a stronger impression of a single entity. In both examples the reason for the striking effect is, I think, the same. Where the words are singular, to turn them into the plural suggests an unexpected burst of feeling; where they are plural, and are fused into a fine-sounding singular, the change in the opposite direction produces an effect of surprise.

CHAPTER 25

Polyptoton: Interchange of Tenses

AGAIN, if you introduce circumstances that are past in time as happening at the present moment, you will turn the passage from mere narrative into vivid actuality. 'Someone,' says Xenophon, 'has fallen under Cyrus's horse, and being trampled on, strikes the horse in the belly with his sword. It rears and throws Cyrus, and he falls to the ground.'[3] Thucydides is particularly fond of this device.

1. *De Corona* 18.
2. Herodotus, VI, 21. Phrynicus was a tragic playwright contemporary with Aeschylus. Herodotus continues the anecdote quoted here by recounting that the Athenians fined Phrynicus 1000 drachmas for reminding them in *The Capture of Miletus* of a disaster which had befallen a friendly state, and ordered that the play should never again be performed.
3. Xenophon, *Cyropaedia* VII, i, 37.

CHAPTER 26

Polyptoton: Variations of Person, or Personal Address

In the same way the change of person is striking, and often makes the hearer feel that he is moving in the thick of the danger:

> You would say that they met in the shock of war, all unwearied and undaunted, so impetuously did they rush into the fray.[1]

Then there is Aratus's

> Do not in that month entrust yourself to the surges of the ocean.[2]

Herodotus does much the same kind of thing: 'From the city of Elephantine you will sail upwards, until you come to a level plain; and after you have crossed this tract, you will board again another ship and sail for two days, and then you will come to a great city whose name is Meroe.'[3] You see, my friend, how, as he takes you in imagination through the places in question, he transforms hearing into sight. All such passages, by their direct personal form of address, bring the hearer right into the middle of the action being described. When you seem to be addressing, not the whole audience, but a single member of it –

> But you would not have known of Tydeus's son for which of the armies he fought –[4]

you will affect him more profoundly, and make him more attentive and full of active interest, if you rouse him by these appeals to him personally.

1. *Iliad* XV, 697–8.
2. Aratus (*fl.* 270 B.C.), one of the didactic poets of Alexandria. This is line 299 of his *Phaenomena*.
3. Herodotus, II, 29.
4. *Iliad* V, 85.

CHAPTER 27

Polyptoton: Conversion to the First Person

AGAIN, there are times when a writer, while speaking of a character, suddenly breaks off and converts himself into that character. A figure of this kind is in a way an outburst of emotion:

> And with a far-echoing shout Hector cried out to the Trojans to rush against the ships and leave the blood-spattered spoils. And if I spy anyone who of his own will holds back from the ships, I will surely bring about his death.[1]

Here the poet has taken upon himself the presentation of the narrative, as is appropriate, and then suddenly, without any warning, has attributed the abrupt threat to the angry chieftain. Had he inserted, 'Hector said so and so', it would have given a frigid effect; as it is, the change in form of the passage has anticipated the sudden change of speakers. Accordingly this figure should be used for preference when a sudden crisis will not give the author time to linger, but compels him to change at once from one character to another.

There is another example in Hecataeus:[2] 'Ceyx took this badly and at once ordered the descendants of Heracles to depart. For it is not in my power to help you. Therefore, in order that you may not perish yourselves and injure me, take yourselves off to some other country.'

In his *Aristogeiton* Demosthenes has by a rather different method used change of person to indicate a rapid play of emotion. 'And will none of you,' he says, 'be found to feel disgust and indignation at the violence of this vile and shameless creature, who – O, you most abandoned of men – whose unbridled speech is not shut in by gates and doors which might well be opened . . . .'[3] With his sense incomplete, he has made

1. *Iliad* XV, 346–9.
2. Hecataeus of Miletus (*fl.* 520 B.C.), historian and geographer.
3. Demosthenes, *Aristogeiton* I, 27.

a sudden change, and in his indignation has all but split a single phrase between two persons – 'who – O, you most abandoned . . .'. Thus, while he has turned his speech round to address Aristogeiton, and seems to have left him out of account,[1] yet with this display of passion he has turned it on him much more forcefully. The same thing occurs in Penelope's speech:

Herald, why have those highborn suitors sent you here? Is it to tell the handmaids of the godlike Odysseus to cease from their labours and prepare a banquet for them? Would that they had never wooed me, nor elsewhere gathered together, that this now were the latest and last of their feasting, you that assemble together and waste so much of our substance, the store of the prudent Telemachus. Nor did you ever in the bygone days of your childhood hear from your fathers what manner of man Odysseus was.[2]

CHAPTER 28

Periphrasis

No one, I think, would dispute that periphrasis contributes to the sublime. For as in music the sweetness of the dominant melody is enhanced by what are known as the decorative additions, so periphrasis often harmonizes with the direct expression of a thought and greatly embellishes it, especially if it is not bombastic or inelegant, but pleasantly tempered.

This is pretty well illustrated by Plato at the beginning of his Funeral Oration:[3] 'We have done what gives them the tribute that is their due, and having gained this, they proceed along their appointed path, escorted publicly by their country, and each man privately by his kinsfolk.' Death, you see, he calls 'their appointed path', and their having been granted the accustomed rites he describes as a kind of 'public escort on the

1. There is an inconsistency here. W. Hamilton Fyfe has in his translation accepted a conjectural emendation which enables him to read, 'while swinging his speech round on to Aristogeiton and appearing to abandon the jury . . . .'

2. *Odyssey* IV, 681–9.

3. Plato, *Menexenus* 236 D.

part of their native land'. Surely he has considerably increased the dignity of his conception here. Has he not made music of the unadorned diction that was his starting-point, and shed over it with something of a tuneful harmony the melodiousness that arises from his periphrasis?

Then there is Xenophon: 'You regard toil as the guide to a life of pleasure; you have garnered in your hearts the best of all possessions and the fittest for warriors. For nothing rejoices you so much as praise.'[1] By rejecting 'you are willing to work hard' in favour of 'you make toil the guide to a life of pleasure', and by expanding the rest of the sentence in the same way, he has added to his eulogy a certain grandeur of thought. And this is true also of that inimitable sentence in Herodotus: 'Upon those Scythians who despoiled her temple the goddess cast a malady that made women of them.'[2]

CHAPTER 29

The Dangers of Periphrasis

HOWEVER, periphrasis is a hazardous business, more so than any other figure, unless it is used with a certain sense of proportion. For it quickly lapses into insipidity, akin to empty chatter and dullness of wit. This is why even Plato, who always uses figures with skill, but sometimes with a certain lack of timeliness, is mocked when he says in his *Laws* that 'neither golden nor silver treasure should be allowed to establish itself and dwell in a city';[3] so that if he had been forbidding people to possess herds, says the critic, he would obviously have said 'ovine and bovine treasure'.

However, my digression on the use of figures and their bearing on the sublime has gone on long enough, my dear Terentianus. They are all means of increasing the animation and the emotional impact of style, and emotional effects play as large a part in the production of the sublime as the study of character does in the production of pleasure.

1. Xenophon, *Cyropaedia* I, v, 12.
2. Herodotus, I, 105.
3. *Laws* 801 B.

CHAPTER 30

The Proper Choice of Diction

SINCE in discourse thought and diction are for the most part mutually interdependent, we must further consider whether any other elements that come under the heading of diction remain to be studied. It is probably superfluous to explain to those who already know it how wonderfully the choice of appropriate and high-sounding words moves and enchants an audience, and to remind them that such a choice is the highest aim of all orators and authors; for of itself it imparts to style, as though to the finest statues, at once grandeur, beauty, mellowness, weight, force, power, and any other worthy quality you can think of, and endows the facts as it were with a living voice. For words finely used are in truth the very light of thought. Yet it would not do to use such grand diction all the time, for to apply great and stately terms to trifling matters would be like putting a big tragic mask on a tiny child. However, in poetry and . . .

(Here four pages of the manuscript are missing)

CHAPTER 31

Familiar Language

. . . very thought-provoking and powerful; so too is Anacreon's 'No longer do I care for the Thracian filly.'[1] In this way also that unusual term employed by Theopompus deserves praise, for by reason of the analogy implied it seems to me to be highly expressive, although Cecilius for some reason finds fault with it: 'Philip,' says Theopompus, 'had a genius for stomaching

1. From a fragment of Anacreon, the sixth-century lyric poet. The word 'filly' used here is derived from a conjectural emendation which is suggested by the context, and which seems appropriate to the point that Longinus is making.

things.' Now the homely term is sometimes much more expressive than elegant diction, for, being taken from everyday life, it is at once recognized, and carries the more conviction from its familiarity. Thus, in connexion with a man whose greedy nature makes him put up patiently and cheerfully with things that are shameful and sordid, the words 'stomaching things' are extremely vivid.[1] Much the same may be said of Herodotus's expressions: 'Cleomenes in his madness cut his own flesh into strips with a dagger until, having made a thorough mince of himself, he perished;' and 'Pythes continued fighting on the ship until he was all cut into shreds.'[2] These expressions are on the very edge of vulgarity, but their expressiveness saves them from actually being vulgar.

CHAPTER 32

Metaphor

WITH regard to the appropriate number of metaphors, Cecilius appears to side with those who lay down that two, or at most three, should be brought together in the same passage. Demosthenes is again the standard in this context. The appropriate occasion for their use is when the emotions come pouring out like a torrent, and irresistibly carry along with them a host of metaphors. 'Men,' he says, 'who are steeped in blood, who are flatterers, who have each of them mutilated the limbs of their own fatherlands, who have pledged their liberty by drinking first to Philip, and now to Alexander, measuring their happiness by their bellies and their basest appetites, and who have uprooted that liberty and that freedom from despotism which were to the Greeks of earlier days the rules and standards of integrity.'[3] Here the orator's indignation against the traitors casts a veil over the number of figurative expressions he has used.

1. Theopompus was a historian of the mid fourth century B.C., a disciple of Isocrates.
2. Herodotus, VI, 75; VII, 181.
3. *De Corona* 296.

Now Aristotle and Theophrastus declare that the following phrases have a softening effect on bold metaphors: 'as if', and 'as it were', and 'if one may put it like this', and 'if one may venture the expression'; for the qualifications, they say, mitigate the boldness. I accept this, but at the same time, as I said when I was talking about rhetorical figures, the timely expression of violent emotions, together with true sublimity, is the appropriate antidote for the number and boldness of metaphors. For the onward rush of passion has the property of sweeping everything before it, or rather of requiring bold imagery as something altogether indispensable; it does not allow the hearer leisure to consider the number of metaphors, since he is carried away by the enthusiasm of the speaker.

Furthermore, in the handling of commonplaces and of description nothing so much confers distinction as a continuous series of metaphors. It is by this means that the anatomy of the human body is superbly depicted in Xenophon,[1] and still more divinely in Plato.[2] The head, says Plato, is a citadel, and the neck is constructed as an isthmus between the head and the breast; and the vertebrae, he says, are set below like pivots. Pleasure tempts men to evil, and the tongue is the touchstone of taste. The heart is the fuel-store of the veins, the fountain from which the blood begins its vigorous course, and it keeps its station in the guard-house of the body. The various passages he calls the lanes. 'And for the thumping of the heart which takes place when danger is imminent or when anger is rising, when it becomes fiery-hot, the gods,' he says, 'have devised some relief by implanting the lungs, which, being soft and bloodless, and pierced inwardly with pores, serve as a kind of buffer, so that when anger boils up in the heart, it may throb against a yielding substance and not be damaged.' The seat of the desires he compares with the women's apartments, and that of anger with the men's. Then the spleen is the napkin of the entrails, from which it is filled with waste matter, and swells and festers. 'And after this,' he says, 'they covered everything over with flesh, which they put there, like felt matting, as a protection against attacks from outside.' And he

1. *Memorabilia* I, iv, 5.
2. The descriptions are drawn from the *Timaeus* 65 C – 85 E.

called the blood the fodder of the flesh, adding that, 'in order to provide nourishment, they irrigated the body, cutting channels as is done in gardens, so that, the body being perforated with conduits, the rivulets of the veins might flow on as though from some never-failing source.' And when the end comes, he says, the cables of the soul, like those of a ship, are loosed, and she is set free. These and innumerable similar metaphors form a continuous succession. But those I have mentioned are enough to show that figurative language is a natural source of grandeur, and that metaphors contribute to sublimity; and also that it is emotional and descriptive passages that most gladly find room for them.

However, it is obvious, even without my stating it, that the use of metaphors, like all the other beauties of style, is liable to lead to excess. In this respect even Plato is severely criticized, on the ground that he is often carried away by a kind of linguistic frenzy into harsh and intemperate metaphors and bombastic allegory. 'For it is not easy to see,' he says, 'that a city needs to be mixed like a bowl of wine, in which the strong, raging wine seethes as it is poured in, but when it is chastened by another god who is sober, its association with such good company turns it into an excellent and temperate drink.'[1] To call water 'a sober god', say the critics, and to describe mixing as 'chastening', is to use the language of some poet who is not in fact sober.

Cecilius, too, has picked on such defects as these, and in the works he has written in praise of Lysias he has actually dared to represent Lysias as being in all respects superior to Plato. But here he has given way to two uncritical impulses; for although he is even fonder of Lysias than of himself, his hatred for Plato altogether surpasses his love for Lysias. However, he is merely being contentious, and his premisses are not, as he thought, admitted. For he prefers the orator, whom he regards as faultless and without blemish, to Plato, who often made mistakes. But this is not the truth of the matter, nor anything like the truth.

1. Plato, *Laws* 773 C.

CHAPTER 33

Superiority of Flawed Sublimity to Flawless Mediocrity

SUPPOSE we take some writer who really may be considered flawless and beyond reproach. In this context we must surely ask ourselves in general terms, with reference to both verse and prose, which is superior, grandeur accompanied by a few flaws, or mediocre correctness, entirely sound and free from error though it may be. Yes, and further, whether in literature the first place should rightly be given to the greater number of virtues, or to virtues which are greater in themselves. For these questions are proper to a study of sublimity, and for every reason they should be resolved.

Now I am well aware that the highest genius is very far from being flawless, for entire accuracy runs the risk of descending to triviality, whereas in the grand manner, as in the possession of great wealth, something is bound to be neglected. Again, it may be inevitable that men of humble or mediocre endowments, who never run any risks and never aim at the heights, should in the normal course of events enjoy a greater freedom from error, while great abilities remain subject to danger by reason of their very greatness. And in the second place, I know that it is always the less admirable aspects of all human endeavours that are most widely noticed; the remembrance of mistakes remains ineradicable, while that of virtues quickly melts away.

I have myself observed a good many faults in Homer and our other authors of the highest distinction, and I cannot say that I enjoy finding these slips; however, I would not call them wilful errors, but rather careless oversights let in casually and at random by the heedlessness of genius. I am none the less certain that the greater virtues, even if they are not consistently shown throughout the composition, should always be voted into the first place – for the greatness of mind that they represent, if for no other reason. Now Apollonius reveals himself in his

Argonautica[1] as an impeccable poet, and Theocritus is extremely successful in his pastorals, apart from a few surface blemishes. Yet would you not rather choose to be Homer than Apollonius?

And again, is Eratosthenes in his *Erigone*,[2] which is an entirely flawless little poem, a greater poet than Archilochus, whose verse is often ill-arranged, but who has surges of a divine inspiration which it would be difficult to bring under the control of rules? Furthermore, would you choose as a lyrical poet to be Bacchylides rather than Pindar? And in tragedy Ion of Chios rather than Sophocles? Bacchylides and Ion are, it is true, faultless and elegant writers in the polished manner. But Pindar and Sophocles seem at times in their impetuous career to burn up everything in their path, although their fire is often unaccountably quenched, and they lapse into a most miserable flatness. Yet would anyone in his senses put the whole series of Ion's works on the same footing as the single play of *Oedipus*?

CHAPTER 34

Hyperides and Demosthenes

If success in composition were not judged according to true standards, then Hyperides would be ranked altogether higher than Demosthenes. For he has more variety of tone than Demosthenes, and more numerous merits. In every branch of his art he is very nearly in the first flight, like the pentathlete; in each contest he is inferior to the champions among his rivals, but comes first among the amateurs.

Now Hyperides not only imitates all the virtues of Demosthenes except his talent in composition; he has also with uncommon success taken to his province the merits and graces of

1. Apollonius Rhodius (*fl.* 240 B.C.) was the foremost Alexandrian epic poet; his *Argonautica*, an epic in four books on the story of Jason and the Argonauts, is extant.

2. Eratosthenes, a versatile Alexandrian author and scholar of the third century B.C. The *Erigone* is an elegy based on the story of Icarius, his daughter Erigone, and his dog Maera.

Lysias. For he talks plainly, when this is required, and does not like Demosthenes make all his points in a monotonous series. He has, too, a gift for characterization, seasoned with charm and simplicity. Moreover, he has considerable wit, a most urbane raillery, true nobility of manner, a ready skill in exchanges of irony, a fund of jokes which, in the Attic manner, are neither tasteless nor ill-bred, but always to the point, a clever touch in satire, and plenty of comic force and pointed ridicule combined with a well-directed sense of fun – and all this invested with an inimitable elegance. He is very well endowed by nature with the power to awaken pity. He is a fluent story-teller, and with his easy flow of inspiration has an excellent faculty for winding his way through a digression, as of course he shows in his somewhat poetic handling of the story of Leto. And he has treated his Funeral Oration as, I think, no one else could have done it.

Demosthenes, on the other hand, is not good at describing character. He is not concise, nor has he any fluency nor any talent for delivering set orations. In general he partakes of none of the merits that have just been listed. When he is forced into attempting a joke or a witticism, he does not so much raise laughter at what he says as make himself the object of laughter, and when he wants to exert a little charm, he comes nowhere near doing so. If he had tried to write the little speeches on Phryne or Athenogenes, he would have made us think even more highly of Hyperides.[1] All the same, in my opinion the virtues of Hyperides, many as they may be, are wanting in the requisite grandeur; the productions of a sober-hearted fellow, they are staid and do not disturb the peace of mind of the audience – certainly no one who reads Hyperides is frightened by him. But when Demosthenes takes up the tale, he displays the virtues of great genius in their highest form: a sublime intensity, lifelike passions, copiousness, readiness, speed, where it is appropriate, and his own unapproachable power and vehemence. Having, I say, made himself master of all the riches of these mighty, heaven-sent gifts – for it would not be right to call them human – he invariably, by reason of the virtues he possesses, puts down all his rivals, and this even where

1. Hyperides's speech against Athenogenes was recovered last century; his defence of Phryne is lost.

the qualities he does not possess are concerned; it might be said, indeed, that he overpowers with his thunder and lightning the orators of every age. One could more easily outface a descending thunderbolt than meet unflinchingly his continual outbursts of passion.

CHAPTER 35

Plato and Lysias

In the case of Plato and Lysias there is, as I have said, a further point of difference. Lysias is much inferior to Plato in both the greatness and the number of his merits, and at the same time he surpasses him in his faults even more than he falls short of him in his virtues.

What then was in the mind of those godlike authors who, aiming at the highest flights of composition, showed no respect for detailed accuracy? Among many other things this – that nature has adjudged us men to be creatures of no mean or ignoble quality. Rather, as though inviting us to some great festival, she has brought us into life, into the whole vast universe, there to be spectators of all that she has created and the keenest aspirants for renown; and thus from the first she has implanted in our souls an unconquerable passion for all that is great and for all that is more divine than ourselves. For this reason the entire universe does not satisfy the contemplation and thought that lie within the scope of human endeavour; our ideas often go beyond the boundaries by which we are circumscribed, and if we look at life from all sides, observing how in everything that concerns us the extraordinary, the great, and the beautiful play the leading part, we shall soon realize the purpose of our creation.

This is why, by some sort of natural instinct, we admire, not, surely, the small streams, beautifully clear though they may be, and useful too, but the Nile, the Danube, the Rhine, and even more than these the Ocean. The little fire that we have kindled ourselves, clear and steady as its flame may be, does not strike us with as much awe as the heavenly fires, in spite of their often being shrouded in darkness; nor do we think it a greater marvel than the craters of Etna, whose eruptions throw up from their depths rocks and even whole mountains, and at times pour out rivers of that pure Titanian fire. In all such circumstances, I would say only this, that men hold cheap what is useful and necessary, and always reserve their admiration for what is out of the ordinary.

CHAPTER 36

Sublimity and Literary Fame

Now with regard to authors of genius, whose grandeur always has some bearing on questions of utility and profit,[1] it must be observed at the outset that, while writers of this quality are far from being faultless, yet they all rise above the human level. All other attributes prove their possessors to be men, but sublimity carries one up to where one is close to the majestic mind of God. Freedom from error escapes censure, but the grand style excites admiration as well. It need scarcely be added that each of these outstanding authors time and again redeems all his failures by a single happy stroke of sublimity; and, most decisive of all, that if we were to pick out all the blunders of Homer, Demosthenes, Plato, and the greatest of all our other authors, and were to put them all together, it would be found that they amounted to a very small part, say rather an infinitesimal fraction, of the triumphs achieved by these demigods on every page. That is why the judgement of all ages, which envy itself cannot convict of perversity, has awarded them the palm of victory, guarding it as their inalienable right, and likely so to preserve it 'as long as rivers run and tall trees flourish'.[2]

As for the writer who maintains that the faulty Colossus is not superior to Polycleitus's spearman, one obvious retort, among many others, is to point out that meticulous accuracy

1. Which is not the case with all the grandeurs of nature named in the previous chapter.
2. Author unknown. Also quoted in a slightly different form as part of a longer quotation in Plato, *Phaedrus* 264 C.

is admired in art, grandeur in the works of nature, and that it is by nature that man is endowed with the power of speech. Moreover, in statues we look for the likeness of a man, whereas in literature, as I have said, we look for something transcending the human. However, to revert to the doctrine with which I began my commentary,[1] since freedom from faults is usually the result of art, and distinction of style, however unevenly sustained, is due to genius, it is right that art should everywhere be employed as a supplement to nature, for in cooperation the two may bring about perfection.

So much it has been necessary to say in order to resolve the problems before us. But everyone is welcome to his own taste.

CHAPTER 37

Comparisons and Similes

CLOSELY related to metaphors – for we must go back to them – are comparisons and similes, which differ only in this....

(*Here two pages of the manuscript are missing*)

CHAPTER 38

Hyperboles

...and such hyperboles as, 'Unless you carry your brains trodden down in your heels'.[2] One must therefore know in each case where to draw the line, for sometimes if one overshoots the mark one spoils the effect of the hyperbole, and if such expressions are strained too far they fall flat, and sometimes produce the opposite effect to that which was intended. Isocrates, for example, unaccountably lapsed into childishness through the ambition which led to his fondness for exaggeration. The theme of his *Panegyric* is that Athens is superior to

1. See Chapter 2.
2. From a work at one time ascribed to Demosthenes, *De Halonneso* 45.

Sparta in the benefits that she has conferred on the Greeks, but at the very beginning he declares: 'Moreover, words have such power that they can make what is grand humble, and endow petty things with greatness; they can express old ideas in a new way, and discuss what has just happened in the style of long ago.'[1] 'Do you then by these means, Isocrates,' says someone, 'intend to interchange the roles of the Athenians and the Spartans?' For in his eulogy of the power of language he has all but made a prefatory announcement to his auditors that he himself is not to be trusted. Perhaps then, as I said earlier about rhetorical figures,[2] the best hyperboles are those which conceal the fact that they are hyperboles. And this happens when, under the influence of powerful emotion, they are used in connexion with some great circumstance, as is the case with Thucydides when he speaks of those who perished in Sicily. 'For the Syracusans,' he says, 'went down and began their slaughter, especially of those who were in the river. And the water was immediately polluted; but none the less it was drunk, thick though it was with mud and blood, and most of them still thought it was worth fighting for.'[3] That a drink of mud and blood should still be worth fighting for is made credible by the height of the emotions excited by the circumstances.

The same is true of Herodotus's account of those who fought at Thermopylae. 'In this place,' he says, 'as they were defending themselves with their daggers, such of them as still had daggers, and with their very hands and mouths, the barbarians buried them.'[4] Here you may ask what is meant by fighting against armed men 'with their very mouths', and being 'buried' with arrows. At the same time the expressions carry conviction, for the incident does not seem to be introduced for the sake of the hyperbole, but the hyperbole seems to take its rise quite plausibly from the incident. For as I keep on saying, actions and feelings which come close to sweeping us off our feet serve as an excuse and a lenitive for any kind of daring phraseology. This is why, even when they reach the point of being

1. Isocrates, *Panegyric* 8.
2. Chapter 17.
3. Thucydides, VII, 84.
4. Herodotus, VII, 255.

actually incredible, the shafts of comedy also seem plausible from their very laughability, as in

The field he had was smaller than a letter.[1]

For laughter, too, is an emotion, related as it is to pleasure.

Hyperboles may apply just as much to petty things as to great, an overstraining of the facts being the common element. In a sense satire is the exaggeration of pettiness.

CHAPTER 39

Composition, or Disposition of Material

THE fifth of the factors contributing to the sublime which I specified at the beginning remains to be dealt with, my friend, and that is the arrangement of the words in due order. On this matter I have already in two treatises given an adequate account of such conclusions as I could reach; for my present purpose I need only add the essential fact that men find in a harmonious arrangement of sounds, not only a natural medium of persuasion and pleasure, but also a marvellous instrument of grandeur and passion. For does not the flute instil certain emotions into those that hear it, seeming to carry them away and fill them with a divine frenzy? Does it not give rhythmic movement, and compel the hearer to conform to the melody and adapt his own movements to this rhythm, even if he is not in the least musical? Then the tones of the harp, in themselves meaningless, often cast a wonderful spell, as you know, by their variations in sound and the throbbing interplay and harmonious blending of the notes struck.

Yet these are mere semblances, spurious counterfeits of the art of persuasion, and not, as I have mentioned, a genuine expression of human nature. Now composition is a kind of harmony of the words which are implanted in man at his birth, and which affect not his hearing alone but his very soul, and it is my belief that it brings out manifold patterns of words, thoughts, deeds, beauty, and melody, all of them originally

1. Author unknown.

born and bred in us; moreover, by the blending of its myriad tones it brings into the hearts of the bystanders the actual emotion of the speaker, and always induces them to share it; and finally it builds up an accumulation of phrases into a grand and harmonious structure. Are we not to believe that by these means it casts a spell on us, and draws our thoughts towards what is majestic and dignified and sublime, and towards any other potentialities which it embraces, gaining a complete mastery over our minds? But it is madness to dispute on matters which are the subject of such general agreement, since experience is sufficient proof.

An idea which appears sublime, and which is certainly to be admired, is that which Demosthenes associates with his decree: 'This decree caused the peril which at that time encompassed the city to pass away just like a cloud.'[1] But its ring owes no less to the harmony than to the thought, for its delivery rests entirely on the dactylic rhythms, which are the noblest of rhythms and make for grandeur – which is why the heroic measure, the most beautiful of known measures, is composed of dactyls. And indeed, if you moved it wherever you liked away from its proper place,[2] and said, 'this decree, just like a cloud, caused the peril at that time to pass away', or if you cut out a single syllable and said, 'caused to pass away like a cloud', you would realize how far the harmony of sound chimes in with the sublimity. For 'just like a cloud' starts off with a long rhythm, consisting of four metrical beats, and if you remove a single syllable and write 'like a cloud', by this abbreviation you at once mutilate the effect of grandeur. And again, if you stretch the phrase out with 'caused to pass away just as if a cloud', the meaning is the same, but it no longer falls on the ear with the same effect because, by the drawing out of the final beats, the sheer sublimity of the passage is robbed of its solidity and of its tension.

1. *De Corona* 188.

2. The awkwardness here is due to corruption in the text, the loss perhaps of a phrase, perhaps of a preceding sentence, which would have indicated that 'it' refers to the last phrase of the decree, 'just like a cloud'. It is difficult to find English equivalents for most of the technicalities of this paragraph.

CHAPTER 40

The Structure of the Sentence

AMONG the chief agents in the formation of the grand style is the proper combination of the constituent members – as is true of the human body and its members. Of itself no single member, when dissociated from any other, has anything worthy of note about it, but when they are all mutually interconnected they make up a perfect whole. Similarly, when the elements of grandeur are separated from one another, they carry the sublimity along with them, dispersing it in every direction; but when they are combined into a single organism, and, moreover, enclosed within the bonds of harmony, they form a rounded whole, and their voice is loud and clear, and in the periods thus formed the grandeur receives contributions, as it were, from a variety of factors. I have, however, sufficiently demonstrated that many writers both of prose and verse who have no natural gift of sublimity, or even of grandeur, and who for the most part employ common and popular words which carry no extraordinary associations, have nevertheless, by merely combining and fitting these words together in the right order, achieved dignity and distinction and an appearance of grandeur – among many others Philistus,[1] for example, Aristophanes at times, and Euripides as a rule.

After the slaughter of his children Heracles says,

> I am stowed to the hatches with woes, and there is no room for more.[2]

The expression is extremely vulgar, but it becomes sublime by reason of its aptness to its setting. If you fit the passage together in any other way, you will realize that Euripides is a poet rather by virtue of his power of composition than of his ideas. Writing of Dirce being dragged away by the bull, he says:

> And wheresoever he chanced to wheel around, he seized and dragged along at once woman or rock or oak, now this, now that.[3]

1. A Sicilian historian of the fourth century.
2. Euripides, *Hercules Furens* 1245.
3. From the lost *Antiope* of Euripides.

This idea is excellent in itself, but gains further strength from the fact that the rhythm is not hurried or as it were carried along on rollers, but the words offer resistance to one another and derive support from the pauses, and take their stand in a firmly-based grandeur.

CHAPTER 41

Some Impediments to Sublimity

WHERE the sublime is concerned nothing has so debasing an effect as broken or agitated rhythms, such as pyrrhics (⏑ ⏑), trochees (– ⏑), and dichorees (– ⏑ – ⏑), which drop right down to the level of dance-music. For all over-rhythmical styles are at once felt to be cheap and affected; the monotonous jingle seems superficial, and does not penetrate our feelings – and the worst of it is that, just as choral lyrics distract the audience's attention from the action of the play and forcibly turn it to themselves, so also an over-rhythmical style does not communicate the feeling of the words, but only of the rhythm. And so there are times when the hearers foresee the likely endings and themselves break in on the speaker, and, as might happen in dancing, they anticipate the steps and finish too soon.

Equally wanting in grandeur are passages which are too close-packed, or cut up into tiny phrases and words with short syllables, giving the impression of being roughly and unevenly held together with pins.

CHAPTER 42

Conciseness

FURTHERMORE, excessive conciseness in expression reduces sublimity, for grandeur is marred when it is too closely compressed. You must take this to mean, not compression that is properly used, but what is entirely broken up into fragments and thus frittered away. For excessive conciseness curtails the sense where brevity goes straight to the point. On the other hand, it is clear that prolixity is lifeless, since it entails an unseasonable length.

CHAPTER 43

Triviality of Expression, and Amplification

THE use of trivial words terribly disfigures passages in the grand style. For example, as far as content is concerned, the storm in Herodotus is marvellously described, but the description contains certain details which are, heaven knows, too far below the dignity of the subject. One might perhaps instance 'when the sea boiled', where the word 'boiled' is so cacophonous as to detract greatly from the sublimity. Then 'the wind,' he says, 'grew fagged'; and 'an unpleasant end' awaited those who were clinging to the wreck.[1] The phrase 'grew fagged' is uncouth, and lacks dignity, and 'unpleasant' is inappropriate to so great a disaster.

Similarly, when Theopompus had given a marvellous account of the Persian King's descent into Egypt, he spoiled the whole description by the use of some trivial words. 'For which city and which tribe of all those in Asia,' he says, 'did not send envoys to the King? And which of the products of the earth or of the beautiful or precious achievements of art was not brought to him as an offering? Were there not many costly coverlets and mantles, purple and white and multi-coloured, many pavilions of gold furnished with all things needful, many robes of state and costly couches? Further, there was silver and gold plate richly wrought, goblets and mixing-bowls, some of which you might have seen studded with jewels, others embellished in a cunning and costly fashion. In addition to these there were countless myriads of weapons, both Greek and barbarian, and beasts of burden beyond number, and sacrificial victims fattened for the slaughter; and many bushels of spices, and bags and sacks and sheets of papyrus and all other useful things; and such a store of preserved flesh from every kind of victim as to

1. Herodotus, VII, 188; VII, 191; VIII, 13.

form piles so large that anyone approaching them from a distance took them for mounds and hills confronting them.'

Here Theopompus runs from the sublime to the trivial where he ought, on the contrary, to have been heightening his effects. By mixing bags and spices and sacks with the wonderful report of the equipment as a whole, he has almost given the impression of a cook-shop. Suppose that among all those decorative objects, among the golden and jewelled mixing bowls, the silver plate, the pavilions of pure gold, and the goblets – suppose that someone had actually brought paltry bags and sacks and placed them in the midst of all these, his action would have produced an effect that offended the eye. Well, in the same way the untimely introduction of such words as these as it were disfigures and debases the description. He could have given a general account, as he speaks of the 'hills' of flesh being built up, and with regard to the rest of the provisions have spoken of wagons and camels and a host of baggage-animals laden with everything that ministers to the luxury and the pleasures of the table; or he could have called them piles of all kinds of grain and of all that conduces to fine cooking and good living; or if he had to put it so explicitly, he could have spoken of all the delicacies of caterers and good cooks.

In sublime passages we ought not to resort to sordid and contemptible terms unless constrained by some extreme necessity. We should use words that suit the dignity of the subject, and imitate nature, the artist who has fashioned man, for she has not placed in full view our private parts or the means by which our whole frame is purged, but as far as possible has concealed them, and, as Xenophon says,[1] has put their passages into the farthest background so as not to sully the beauty of the whole figure.

However, there is no urgent need to enumerate and classify the things that lead to triviality. For as I have previously indicated the qualities that furnish style with nobility and sublimity, it is obvious that their opposities will for the most part make it mean and ugly.

1. *Memorabilia* I, iv, 6.

CHAPTER 44

The Decay of Eloquence

HOWEVER, as in view of your love of learning I will not hesitate to add, my dear Terentianus, there remains to be cleared up a problem to which a certain philosopher has recently applied his wits. 'I wonder,' he said, 'as no doubt do many other people, why it is that in our age there are men well fitted for public life who are extremely persuasive, who are keen and shrewd, and especially well endowed with literary charm, and yet really sublime and transcendent natures are, with few exceptions, no longer produced. Such a great and world-wide dearth of literature attends our age! Are we,' he went on, 'are we to accept the well-worn view that democracy is the kindly nurse of great men, and that great men of letters may be said to have flourished only under democracy and perished with it? For freedom, they say, has the power to foster the imaginations of high-souled men and to inspire them with hope, and with it there spreads the keenness of mutual rivalry and an eager competition for the first place. Furthermore, by reason of the prizes which are open to all in republics, the intellectual gifts of orators are continually sharpened by practice and as it were kept bright by rubbing, and, as might be expected, these gifts, fostered in freedom, help to shed light on the affairs of state. Nowadays,' he continued, 'we seem to absorb from our childhood onwards the lessons of the slavery to which we are accustomed, all but swaddled in the infancy of our minds as we are in slavish customs and observances, and never tasting of the finest and most productive source of eloquence, by which I mean freedom; and thus we emerge as nothing but sublime flatterers.'

This, he maintained, was the reason why, although all other faculties may fall to the lot even of menials, no slave ever becomes an orator; for the fact that he has no freedom of speech, that he lives as it were a dungeoned life, and that he is always liable to be beaten, comes bubbling up to the surface. As Homer puts it, 'The day of our enslavement takes away half our manhood.'[1] 'And so,' went on the philosopher, 'just as the cages in which they keep the Pygmies, or dwarfs, as they call them, not only stunt the growth of these who are imprisoned in them, if what I hear is true, but also shrink them by reason of the fetters fixed round their bodies, so all slavery, however just it may be, could well be described as a cage of the soul, a common prison-house.'

However, I took him up and said: 'It is easy, my good sir, and a characteristic of human nature, always to be finding fault with the present state of affairs. But consider whether it may be that it is not the peace of this world of ours that corrupts great natures, but much rather this endless war which holds our desires in its grasp, yes, and further still the passions that garrison our lives nowadays and utterly devastate them. For the love of money, that insatiable craving from which we all now suffer, and the love of pleasure make us their slaves, or rather, one might say, sink our lives (body and soul) into the depths, the love of money being a disease that makes us petty-minded, and the love of pleasure an utterly ignoble attribute.

'On further reflection, indeed, I do not see how, if we value the possession of unlimited wealth, or, to give the truth of the matter, make a god of it, we can avoid allowing the evils that naturally attend its entry into our souls. For vast and unlimited wealth is closely followed – step by step, as they say – by extravagance, and no sooner has the one opened the gates of cities and houses than the other comes in and joins it in setting up house there. With the passing of time, according to the philosophers, they build nests in our lives, and soon set about begetting offspring, giving birth to pretentiousness, vanity, and luxury – no bastards these, but very much their true-born issue. And if these children of wealth are allowed to reach maturity they soon breed in our hearts implacable masters, insolence and lawlessness and shamelessness. This will inevitably happen, and then men will no longer lift up their eyes nor take any further thought for their good name; the ruin of their lives will gradually be completed as their grandeur of soul withers and fades until it sinks into contempt, when they become lost in

1. *Odyssey* XVII, 332.

admiration of their mortal capabilities and neglect to develop the immortal.

'A man who has accepted a bribe for a verdict would never be a sound and unbiased judge of what is just and honourable, for a corrupt judge must necessarily regard his own private interests as honourable and just. And where bribery now governs all our lives, and we hunt others to death, and lay traps for legacies, and bargain our souls for gain from any and every source, having become slaves to [luxury], can we expect, in this pestilential ruin of our lives, that there should still remain an unbiased and incorruptible judge of works which possess grandeur or enduring life, and that he would not be overcome by his passion for gain? For such men as we are, indeed, it is perhaps better that we should be ruled than live in freedom. If we were given complete liberty, like released prisoners, our consuming greed for out neighbours' possessions might set the world on fire with our deeds of evil.'

In short, I maintained that what wears down the spirit of the present generation is the apathy in which, with few exceptions, we all pass our lives; for we do no work nor show any enterprise from any other motives than those of being praised or being able to enjoy our pleasures – never from an eager and honourable desire to serve our fellows.

'It is best to leave such things at a guess',[1] and to pass on to the next problem, that is, the emotions, about which I previously undertook to write in a separate treatise, for they seem to me to share a place in literature generally, and especially in the sublime . . .

(*The rest is lost*)

1. Euripides, *Electra* 379.

MORE ABOUT PENGUINS, PELICANS AND PUFFINS